Autism & PDD™ Concept Development
Toys & Entertainment

by Pam Britton Reese and Nena C. Challenner

Skills
- concept development
- language

Ages
- 3 through 8

Grades
- PreK through 3

Evidence-Based Practice

- Early intervention that addresses skill acquisition in the areas of interaction, attention, play, comprehension, and expression will support the development of an even profile. The acquisition of key developmental skills supports the later development of communication, language, and speech and enhances emotional, social, and academic development (RCSLT, 2005).

- Many children with autism spectrum disorders learn more readily through the visual modality (RCSLT, 2005).

- Students need to understand semantic connections among words for academic success (NRP, 2000).

- Vocabulary intervention should provide opportunities for students to use target words in multiple contexts (Boone et al., 2007).

Autism & PDD Concept Development: Toys & Entertainment incorporates these principles and is also based on expert professional practice.

References

Boone, K., Letsky, S., Wallach, S., Young, J., Gingrass, K., & Daly, C. (2007, November 28). *Role of SLP: A method of inclusion.* Paper presented at the 2007 ASHA National Convention. Retrieved March 24, 2009 from http://convention.asha.org/2007/handouts/1137_1371Letsky_Sarah__107277_Nov28_2007_Time_071812AM.ppt

National Reading Panel (NRP). (2000). *Teaching children to read: An evidence-based assessment of the scientific research literature on reading and its implications for reading instruction—Reports of the subgroups.* Retrieved March 24, 2009 from www.nichd.nih.gov/publications/nrp/upload/report.pdf

Royal College of Speech & Language Therapists (RCSLT). (2005). *Clinical guidelines for speech and language therapists.* Retrieved March 24, 2009 from www.rcslt.org/resources/clinicalguidelines

LinguiSystems

LinguiSystems, Inc.
3100 4th Avenue
East Moline, IL 61244
800-776-4332

FAX: 800-577-4555
Email: service@linguisystems.com
Web: linguisystems.com

Copyright © 2001 LinguiSystems, Inc.

All of our products are copyrighted to protect the fine work of our authors. You may only copy the student materials as needed for your own use. Any other reproduction or distribution of the pages in this book is prohibited, including copying the entire book to use as another primary source or "master" copy.

Printed in the U.S.A.

ISBN 10: 0-7606-0391-X
ISBN 13: 978-0-7606-0391-8

About the Authors

Pam Britton Reese, M.A., CCC-SLP, owns a private practice, CommunicAid Plus, where she provides speech and language services to children and adults. She is also an educational consultant to public and private schools. Pam has over nine years experience in the schools as a speech-language pathologist and teacher of the hearing-impaired. She has worked with children with autism and PDD since 1995. *Autism & PDD: Concept Development* is her fourth publication with LinguiSystems.

Nena C. Challenner, M.Ed., is a Community-Based Instruction Teacher and Inclusion Specialist. She has been a teacher for over 15 years and has taught preschool through second grade. She has worked with children with autism and PDD since 1995. Nena is also a reading consultant at CommunicAid Plus. *Autism & PDD: Concept Development* is her third publication with LinguiSystems.

Dedication

For the children at CommunicAid Plus (CAP Kids!)

Edited by Lauri Whiskeyman
Illustrations by Margaret Warner
Page Layout by Christine Buysse and Lisa Parker

Table of Contents

Introduction 5

    Ball 9

    Doll 21

    Bubbles 33

    Blocks 45

    Play Dough 57

    Puppet 69

    Balloon 81

    Sandbox 93

    Swing 105

    Slide 117

Extension Activities 129

Suggested Literature 139

Picture Communication Symbols (PCS) © 1981-2000.
Reprinted with the permission of Mayer-Johnson, Inc., P.O. Box 1579,
Solana Beach, CA 92075-7579, 1-800-588-4548, *www.mayer-johnson.com*

big	page 48
bottom	page 125
different	pages 49 and 61
in	pages 94, 96, 97, and 100
little	page 48
top	page 124

Introduction

In our work with children with autism, we were often surprised at misconceptions our students had about the world. For example, when 9-year-old Katie was asked, "What would you do if you saw a house on fire?" she answered, "Roast marshmallows." She had only experienced fire in this way and was unable to perceive that fire might also be dangerous, that it burns, or that it can heat a home. Other children with autism whom we have known didn't recognize a sitting dog as a dog or a rocking chair as a chair. These are concepts that typically-developing children are able to process through observing or listening to information and instantly linking to other learned concepts. We know that children with autism must be taught such language skills as naming attributes, placing words in appropriate categories, and giving descriptions.

It is well documented that children with autism learn more easily when information is presented in a visual format. The picture is constant and the child can view it until the concept is learned, as opposed to the transient nature of speech. Most books published for young children, however, do not teach the concepts the child with autism needs to learn. Although the stories are often engaging and the artwork of museum quality, they too often confuse the child with autism. Foxes that drive? Animals that wear clothing and talk? Cars with eyes? Although amusing, they are not a realistic depiction of our world. Often, too, the art is very complex with many extraneous details. (A list of some books we found that did a good job of teaching concepts is included on page 139.)

Each book in *Autism & PDD: Concept Development* covers 10 concepts around a theme:

- Animals
- Clothing
- Food
- Household Items
- Toys and Entertainment
- Transportation

Specific attributes and features of each concept are illustrated with large pictures, simple sentences, and picture symbols. The sentences describe larger pictures illustrating specific features and attributes of a concept. In addition, there are questions to check comprehension and activities to help the child apply this knowledge to other contexts. These books were developed for professionals who work with children with autism, ages 3 through 8. However, these books can also be used with children who have language delays or language disorders caused by disabilities such as Down syndrome. Parents and caregivers can also use these books.

How to Use this Book

This book contains concepts about 10 different toys and forms of entertainment. Each concept is illustrated in both a large-page and mini-page format for making books to read to the child. We suggest that the large-page format be copied. Place the pages in plastic page protectors. Sliding a thin piece of cardboard or card stock into the pocket between the pages will stiffen the

Introduction, continued

pages and make them easier for young children to turn. Put the pages into folders with brads or three-ring notebooks to create a book. You may want to put a copy of the first page of each unit on the front of the folder or notebook. The mini-pages can be made into small books for the children to take home after they've heard the story at school.

You may want to use all of the concepts in the book at one time to introduce or extend a thematic unit or you can select a specific concept to focus on. For example, a child might know dog and cat, but have no idea what a rabbit is! Remember to go at the child's pace. A child might need many lessons on chairs, for example, before moving on to other concepts in the book.

Comprehension Questions

A variety of comprehension questions (e.g., *yes-no, wh-, how*) follow each concept. The questions can be used in different ways. Some children may only be able to answer the *yes-no* questions. Some children may do better with the *wh-* and *how* questions. You can ask the questions after each concept is taught or after each page. If a child has difficulty answering a question, go through the targeted concept again and help him or her find the answer. Cue the child by pointing to the picture and/or text as you ask the question again.

Generalization Pages

Each concept has a generalization exercise. This exercise is designed to check the child's comprehension of the concept as well as to extend understanding of the concept to different forms and views. Many of the children we work with understand only one form of a concept: "That is a cat. That cat is gray. Thus, all cats must be gray or they are not cats." As you can see, that is a false generalization. By presenting variations of the same concept such as size, color, and position, the child learns to expand his or her mental definition of the concept.

After you read about the targeted concept, make a copy of the generalization page for the child. Read the directions aloud and have the child complete the page. Then encourage the child to describe the circled concepts. Depending on the child's level, the responses could be as simple as labeling "shirt" or as elaborate as "The shirt has long sleeves." You can also use the pictures on this page to point out the differences between the circled concepts.

Extension Activities

The activities suggested at the end of the book give the child the opportunity to experience the new concepts in a natural setting. Although children with autism learn concepts more easily in a visual format that never changes (e.g., the generalization pages), it is equally important to give the child the opportunity to taste that apple or see the balloon fly around the room. Each activity page contains a list of materials needed to complete the activity, instructions for the adult, and Picture Prompt Cards. The Picture Prompt Cards may be used in a variety of ways. Some suggestions are:

Introduction, continued

1. Copy the cards and glue them onto index cards or put them on a communication board. Use them to prompt the appropriate behaviors in each activity.

2. Make two copies of each card and use for a matching game.

3. Copy the cards to send home for families to repeat the activities at home.

Suggested Literature

We have included a list of children's literature to help extend and promote generalization of the concepts to other contexts. These books were carefully chosen because of their simple text and realistic pictures. It is important to provide as many opportunities as possible for the child with autism to see and hear the concept. We have found that repeated exposure to the concepts in *Autism & PDD: Concept Development*, followed by other books with different pictures and texts, aids the child with autism in generalizing the concept to different contexts.

Closing

Remember that the concepts covered in the book can be taught in classrooms as well as group or individual therapy sessions. We hope that the children you work with enjoy the books as much as our students and clients do.

Pam and Nena

A ball is a toy.

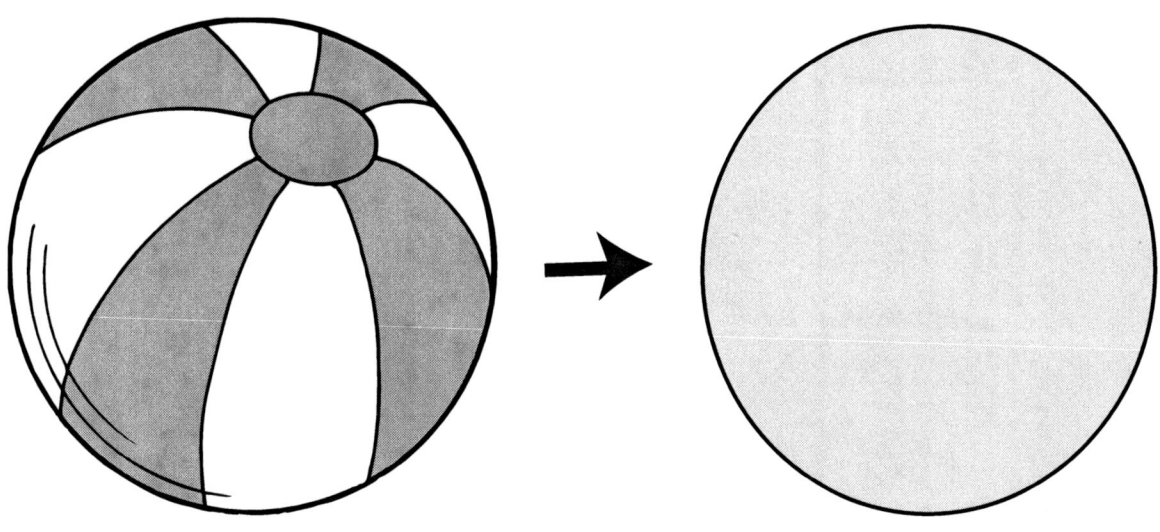

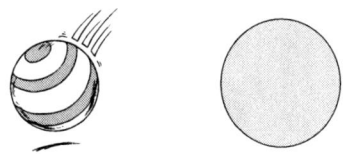

A ball is round.

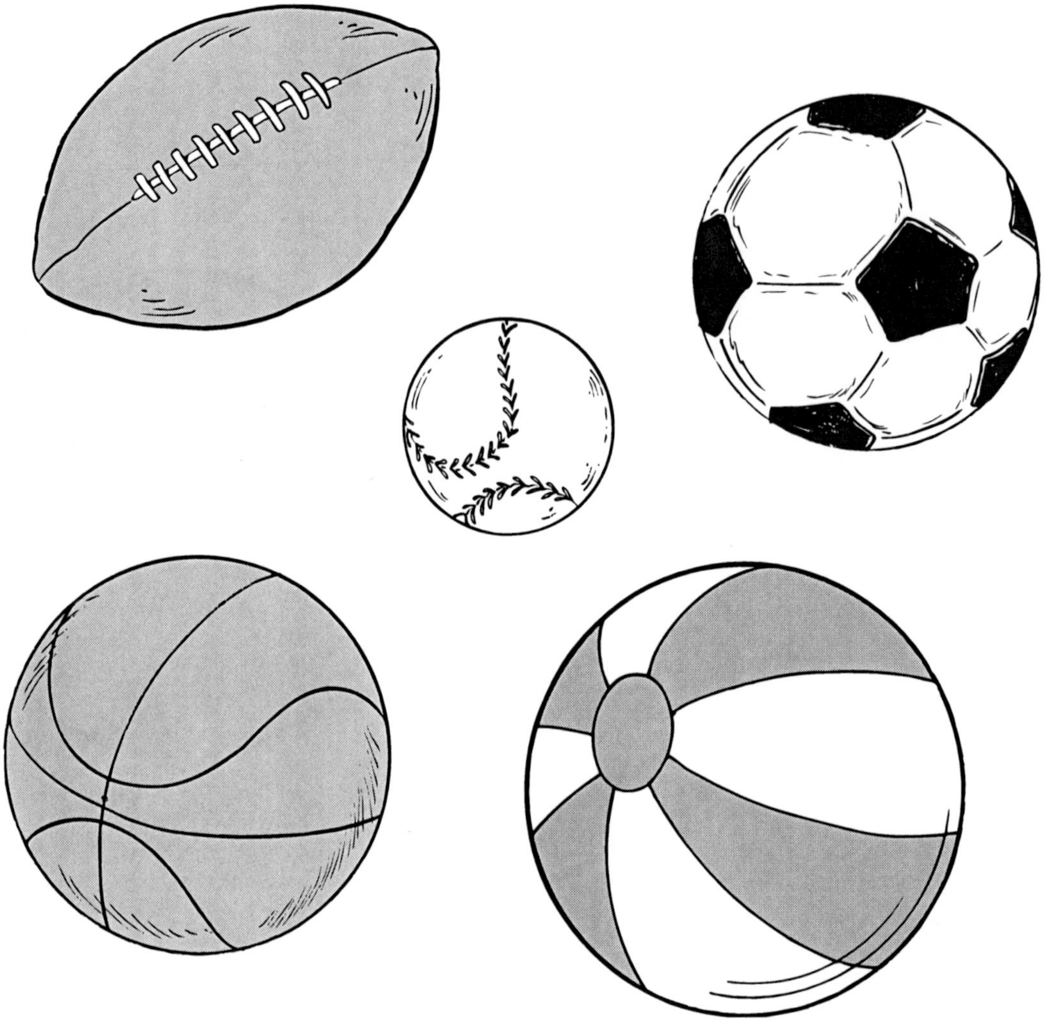

All of these are balls.

Children can roll a ball.

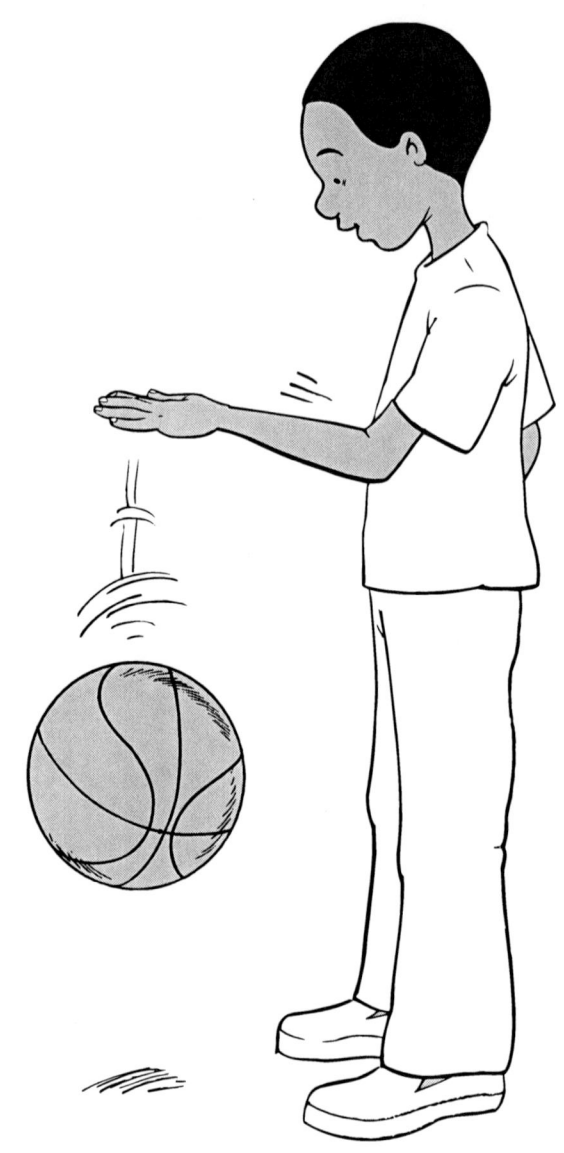

Children can bounce a ball.

Children can throw a ball.

Children can catch a ball.

Children can kick a ball.

Concept: Ball

Yes-No Questions

1. Is a ball a toy?
2. Is a ball square?
3. Do people kick balls?
4. Do people throw balls?
5. Can you eat a ball?
6. Is a ball furniture?
7. Can you catch a ball?
8. Do balls bounce?
9. Do you have a ball?
10. Do you like to throw balls?

Wh- and How Questions

1. What is a ball?
2. What shape is a ball?
3. Who can throw a ball?
4. Who can bounce a ball?
5. Why does a ball roll?
6. Where do people play with balls?
7. What can people kick?
8. What can people catch?
9. How do you play with a ball?
10. When do you play with a ball?

Ball Generalization Page

Circle the balls. Put an X on each picture that is not a ball.

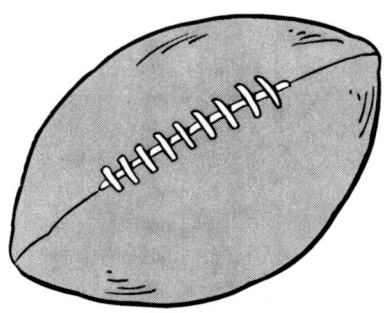

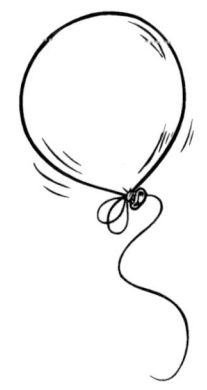

Ball Mini-Book

Copy this page. Cut apart the boxes on the dotted lines. Put the story in order to make a little book and staple.

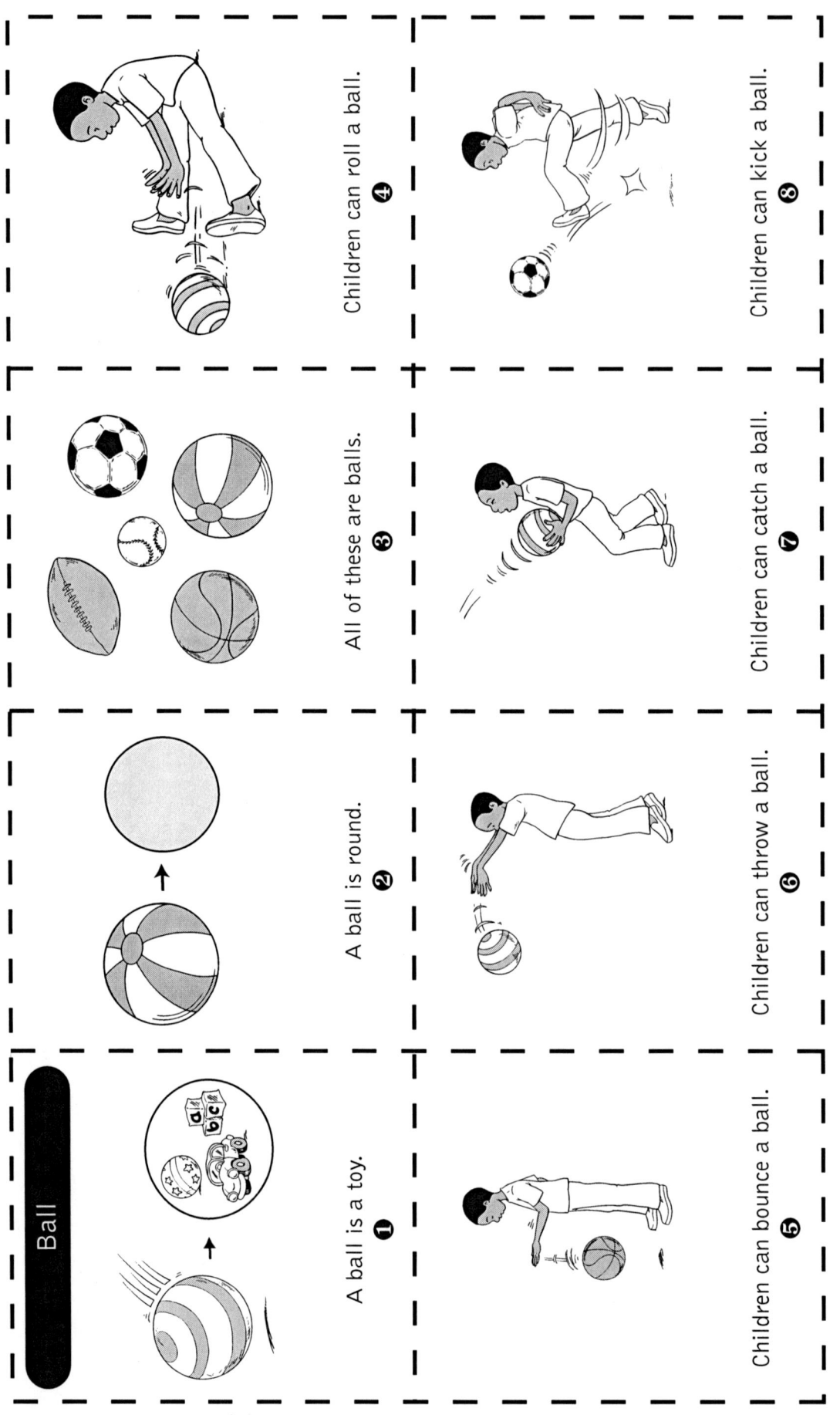

A doll is a toy.

All of these are dolls.

Children play with dolls.

Doll

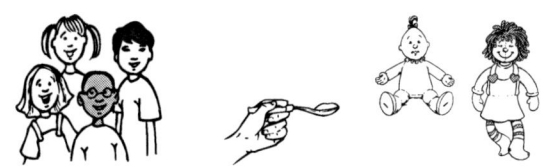

Children feed dolls.

  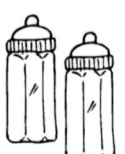 

Children give bottles to dolls.

Children dress dolls.

Children rock and sing to dolls.

Children put dolls to bed.

Concept: Doll

Yes-No Questions

1. Is a doll an animal?
2. Do children play with dolls?
3. Do children color dolls?
4. Do children feed dolls?
5. Is a doll a person?
6. Is a doll a toy?
7. Do children sing to dolls?
8. Can you give a doll a bottle?
9. Do children put dolls to bed?
10. Do you have a doll?

Wh- and How Questions

1. Who does a doll look like?
2. What is a doll?
3. What do children give dolls?
4. Where do children put dolls to sleep?
5. What do children play with?
6. What do dolls wear?
7. Who has a doll?
8. How do you dress a doll?
9. How do you wash a doll?
10. What is your doll's name?

Doll Generalization Page

Circle the dolls. Put an X on each picture that is not a doll.

Doll
Concept Development: Toys & Entertainment

Doll Mini-Book

Copy this page. Cut apart the boxes on the dotted lines. Put the story in order to make a little book and staple.

1. A doll is a toy.
2. All of these are dolls.
3. Children play with dolls.
4. Children feed dolls.
5. Children give bottles to dolls.
6. Children dress dolls.
7. Children rock and sing to dolls.
8. Children put dolls to bed.

Bubbles

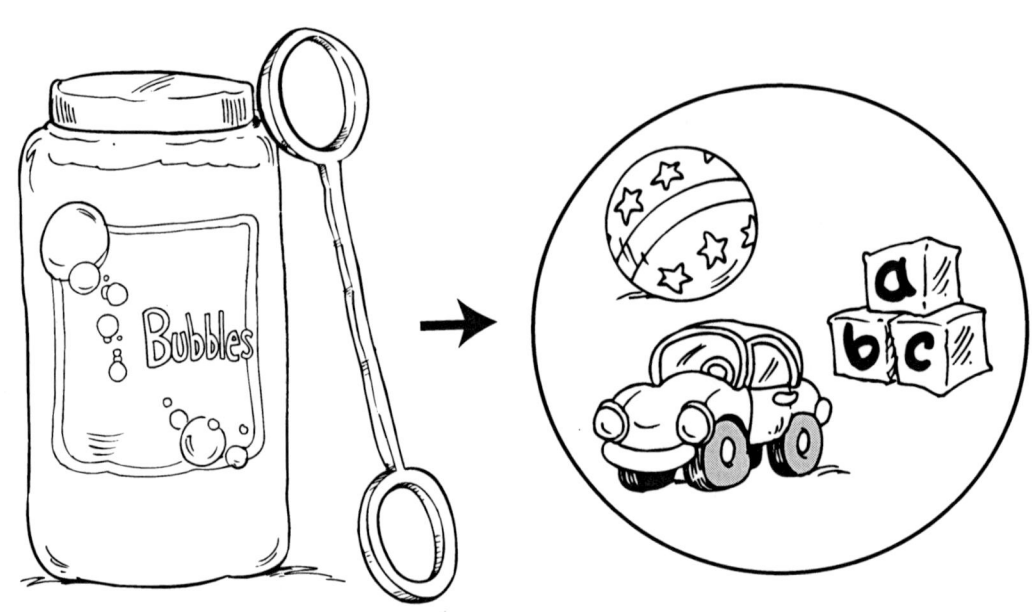

Bubbles are a toy.

Children play with bubbles.

Children blow bubbles with a wand.

Bubbles are soapy.

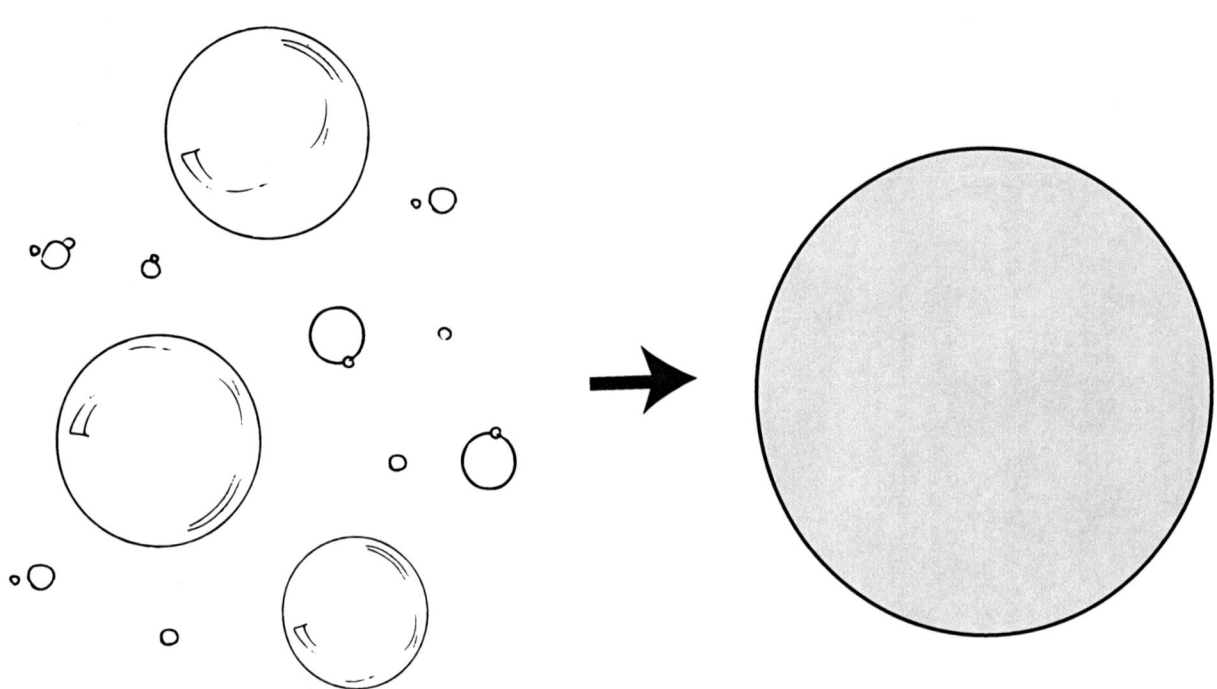

Bubbles are round.

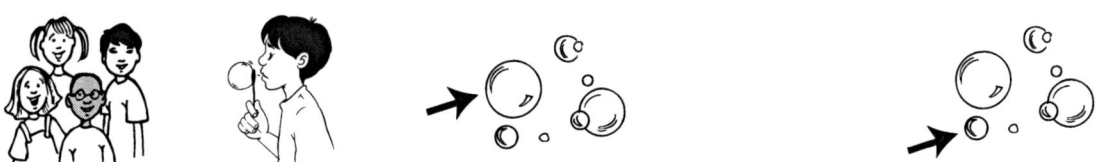

Children blow big bubbles and little bubbles.

Bubbles float in the air.

Bubbles pop.

Concept: Bubbles

Yes-No Questions

1. Are bubbles a food?
2. Do children play with bubbles?
3. Are bubbles square?
4. Do bubbles float?
5. Are bubbles dirty?
6. Are bubbles soapy?
7. Do bubbles pop?
8. Do children eat bubbles?
9. Do children blow bubbles?
10. Do you like bubbles?

Wh- and How Questions

1. Who plays with bubbles?
2. What shape are bubbles?
3. How do you pop a bubble?
4. Where do bubbles float?
5. How do you make bubbles?
6. What do you do with a wand?
7. What are bubbles made of?
8. What size are bubbles?
9. Where do children blow bubbles?
10. Why do bubbles pop?

Bubbles Generalization Page

Circle the bubbles. Put an X on each picture that does not show bubbles.

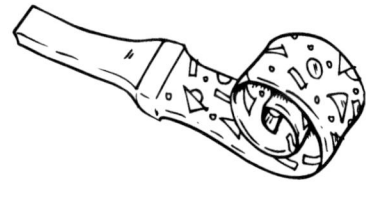

Bubbles Mini-Book

Copy this page. Cut apart the boxes on the dotted lines. Put the story in order to make a little book and staple.

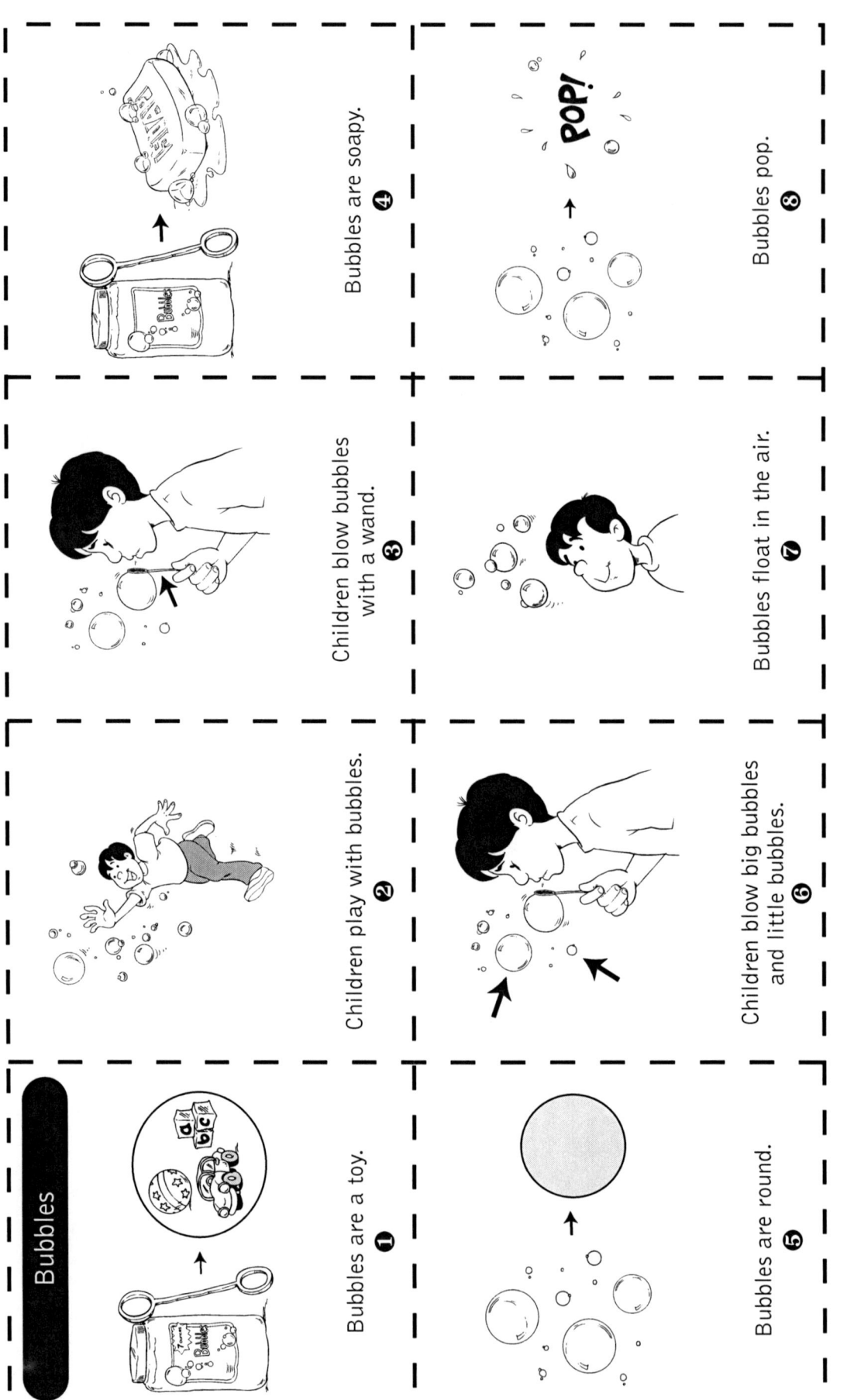

Bubbles

Concept Development: Toys & Entertainment

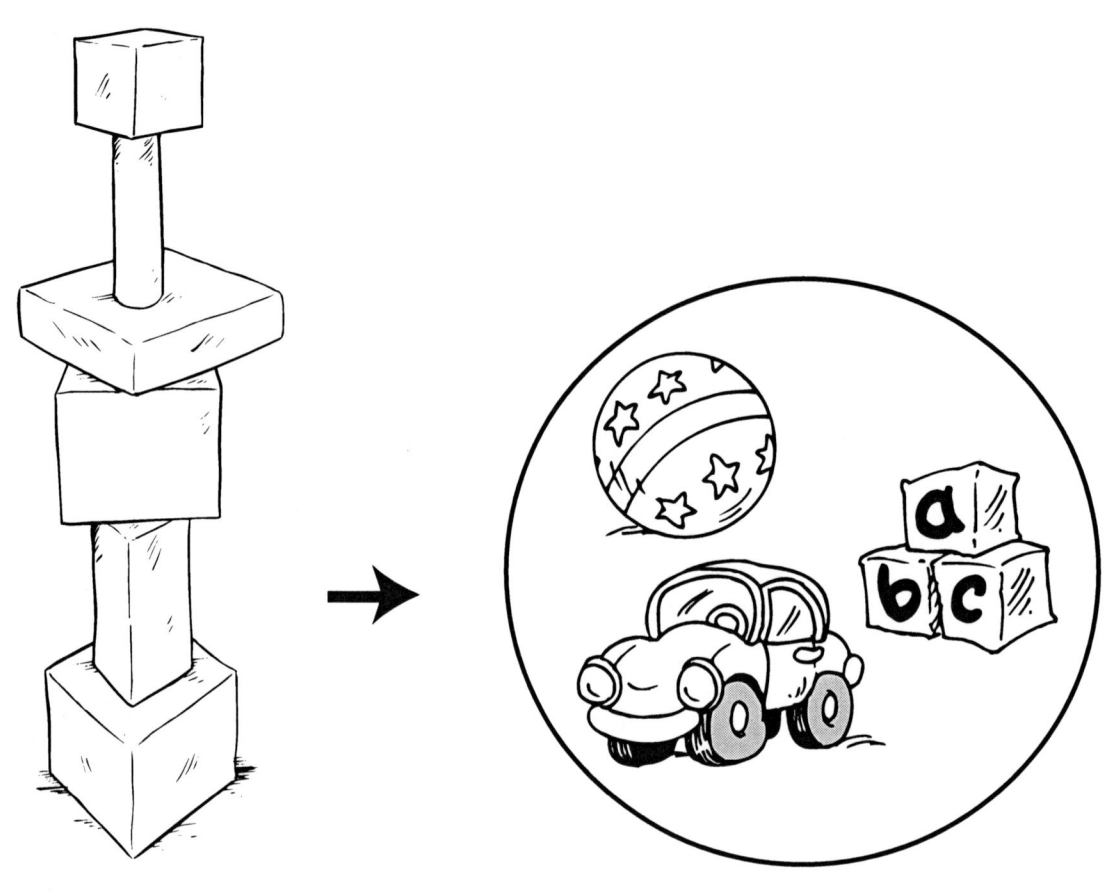

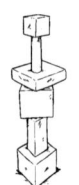 

Blocks are a toy.

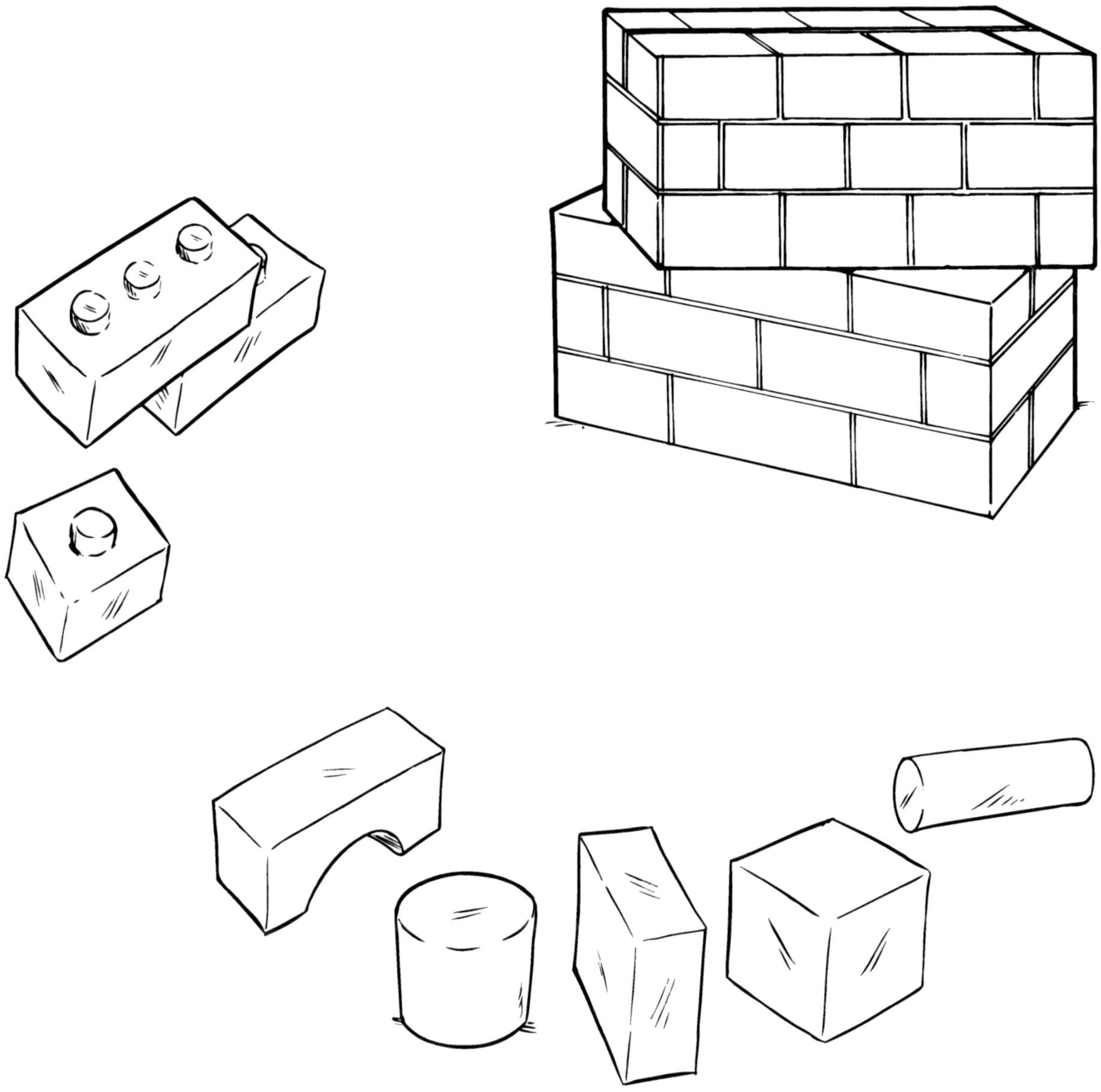

All of these are blocks.

Blocks

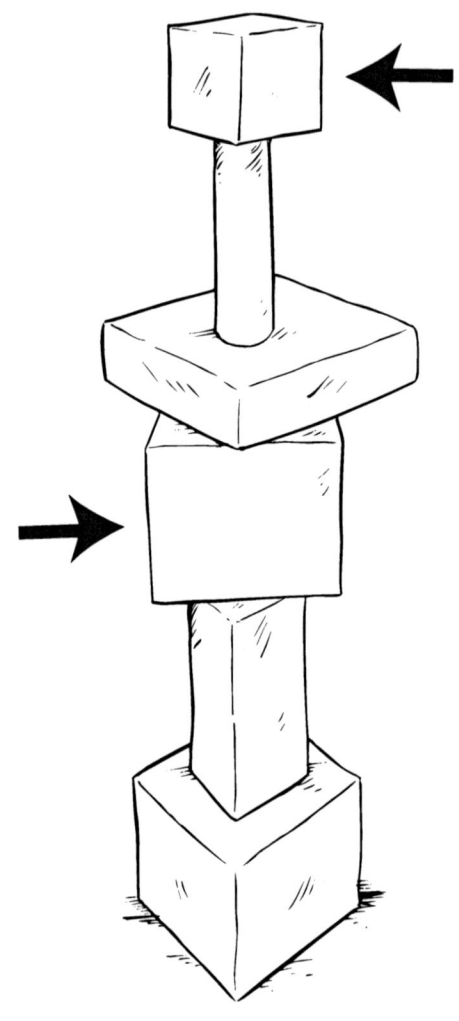

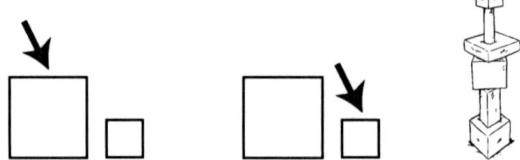
There are big and little blocks.

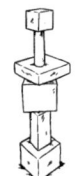  

Blocks are different shapes.

Children play with blocks.

Children build with blocks.

Children stack blocks.

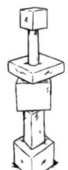 

Sometimes blocks fall down.

Concept: Blocks

Yes-No Questions

1. Are blocks a food?
2. Are blocks a toy?
3. Do children play with blocks?
4. Are all blocks square?
5. Do children build with blocks?
6. Do children feed blocks?
7. Are some blocks little?
8. Can blocks fall down?
9. Do you have blocks?
10. Do you stack blocks to make a tower?

Wh- and How Questions

1. What size are blocks?
2. What shape are blocks?
3. Who builds with blocks?
4. What can you do with blocks?
5. What toy can make a tower?
6. What are blocks?
7. Who plays with blocks?
8. What do children stack?
9. How do you stack blocks?
10. Why do blocks fall down?

Blocks Generalization Page

Circle the blocks. Put an X on each picture that does not show blocks.

Blocks Mini-Book

Copy this page. Cut apart the boxes on the dotted lines. Put the story in order to make a little book and staple.

Play Dough

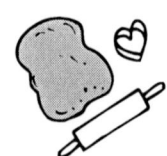 

Play dough is a toy.

Children play with play dough.

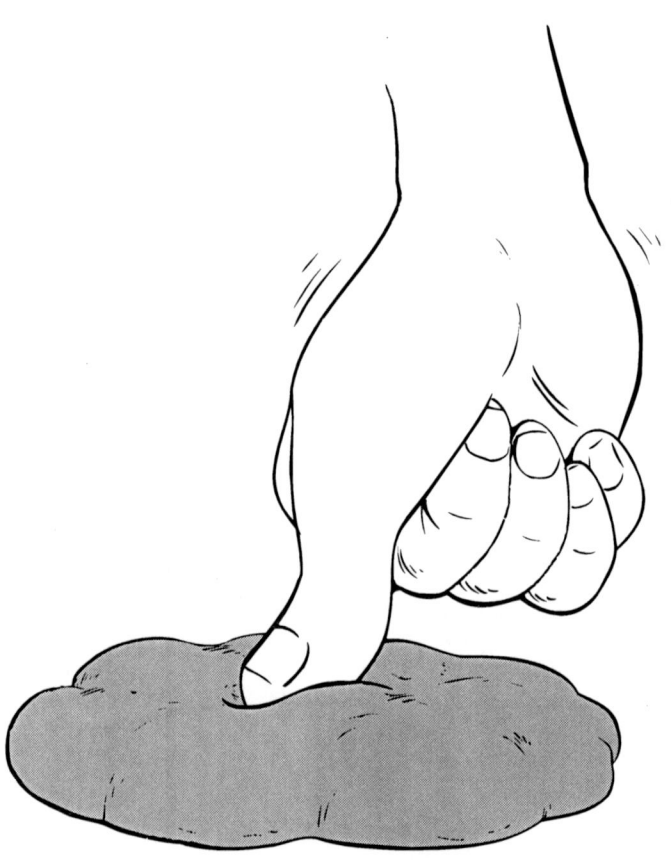

Play dough is soft and squishy.

Play dough is different colors.

Children roll play dough.

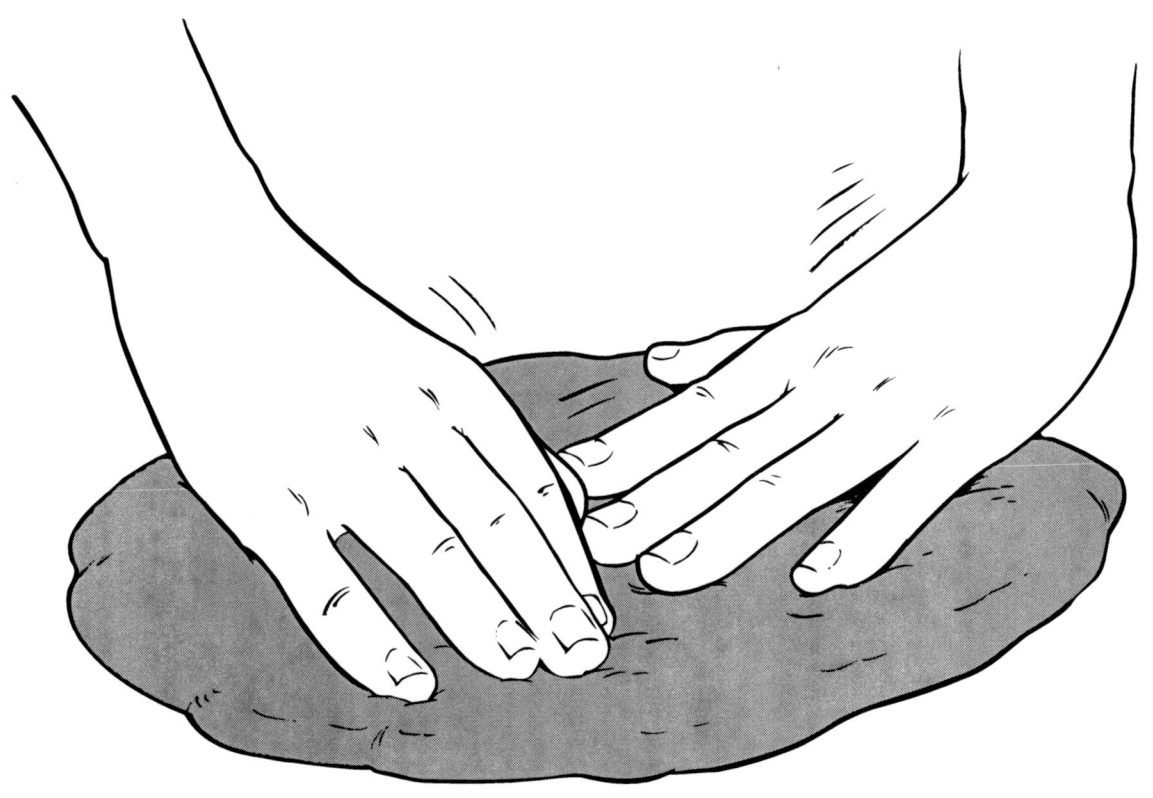

Children pat play dough.

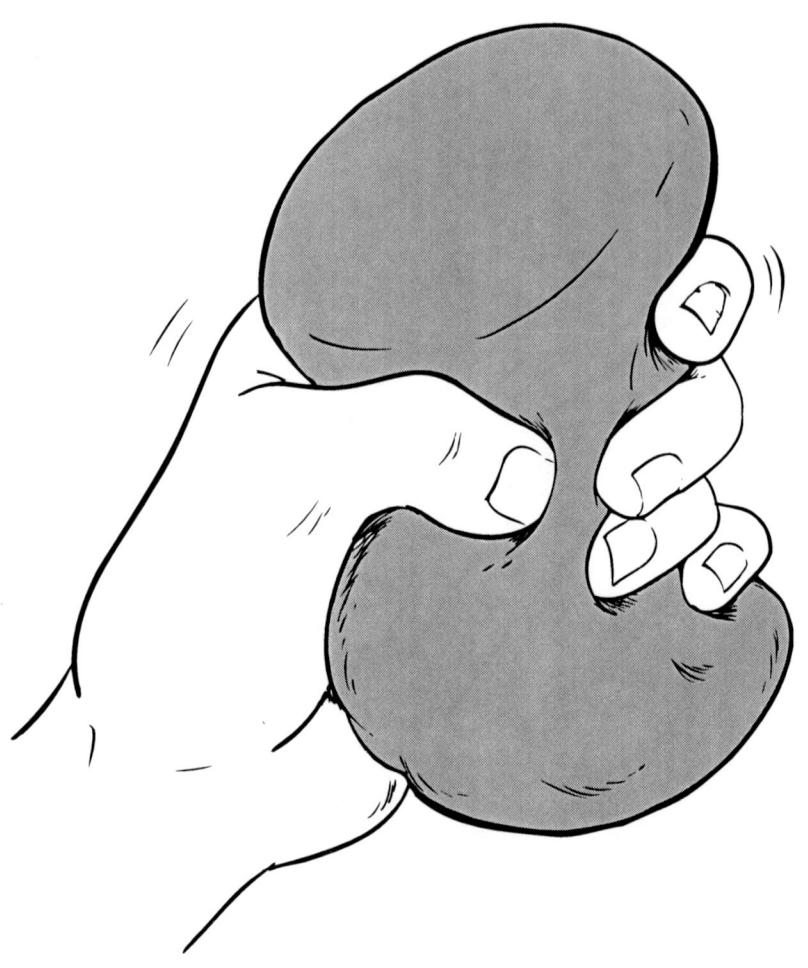

Children squeeze play dough.

Children cut out shapes with play dough.

Concept: Play Dough

Yes-No Questions

1. Is play dough a clothing?
2. Is play dough a toy?
3. Is play dough hard?
4. Is play dough soft?
5. Is play dough sticky?
6. Is play dough red?
7. Do children roll play dough?
8. Do children drink play dough?
9. Do children squeeze play dough?
10. Can you cut play dough?

Wh- and How Questions

1. How does play dough feel?
2. Who plays with play dough?
3. What color is play dough?
4. What can you roll?
5. Where do you play with play dough?
6. What can you squeeze?
7. What do children pat?
8. Where do you keep play dough?
9. What color of play dough do you like?
10. What do you use to squeeze play dough?

Play Dough Generalization Page

Circle the play dough. Put an X on each picture that is not play dough.

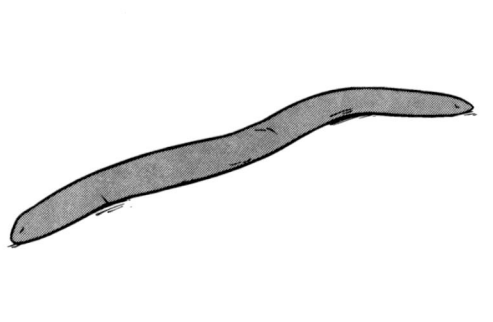 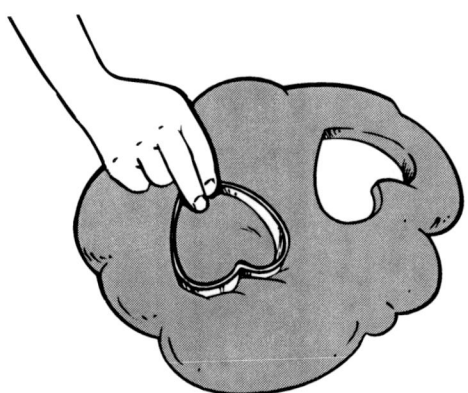

Play Dough Mini-Book

Copy this page. Cut apart the boxes on the dotted lines. Put the story in order to make a little book and staple.

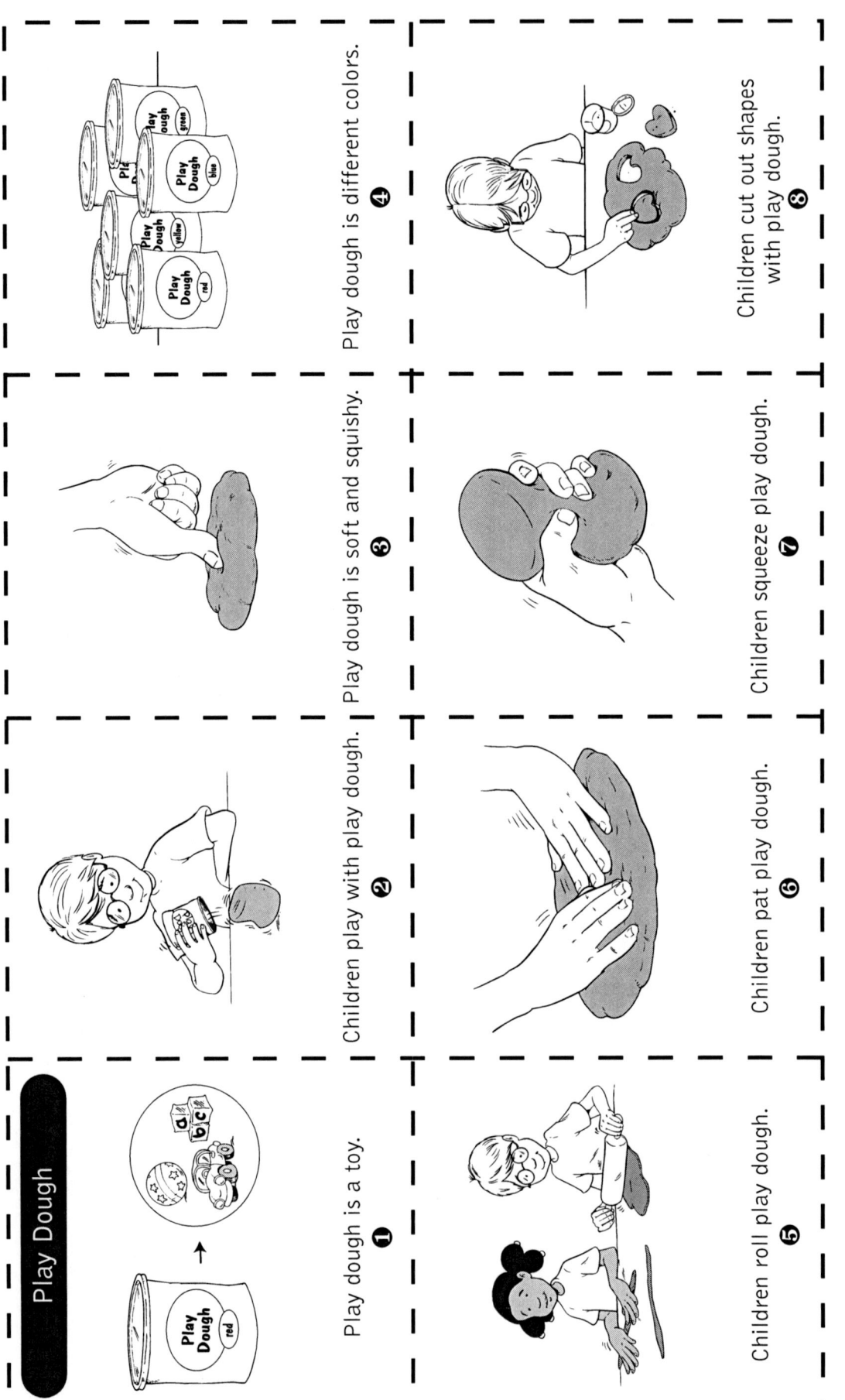

Puppet

A puppet is a toy.

Children play with puppets.

Some puppets look like little animals.

Some puppets look like little people.

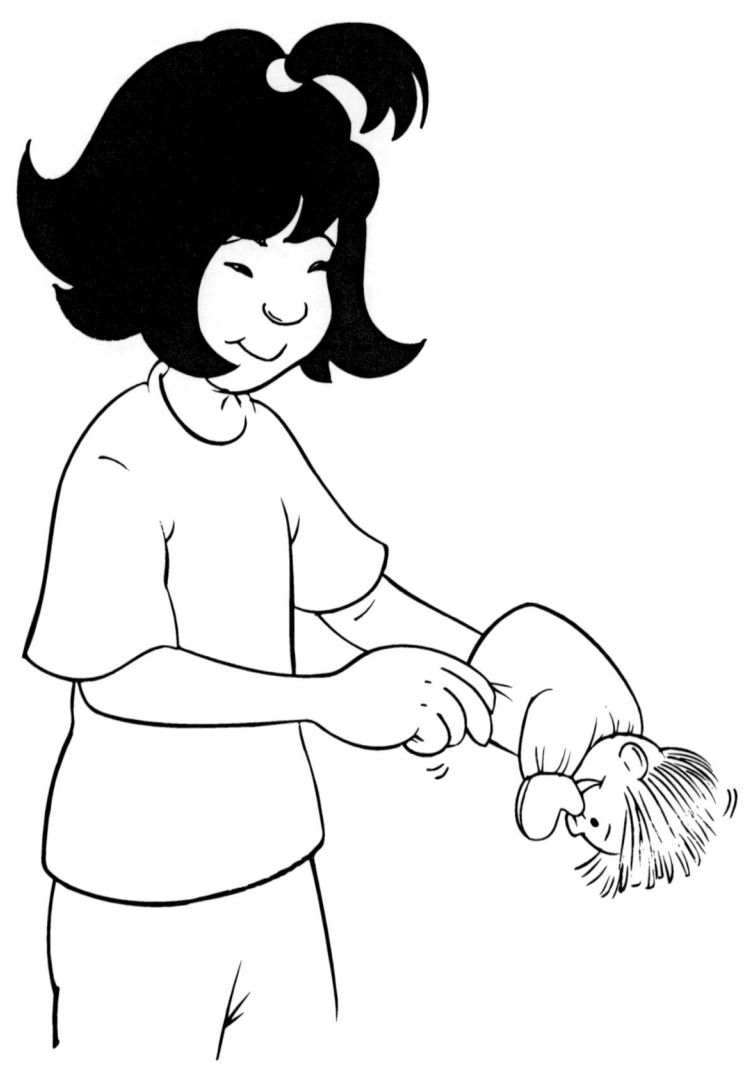

Children put puppets on their hands.

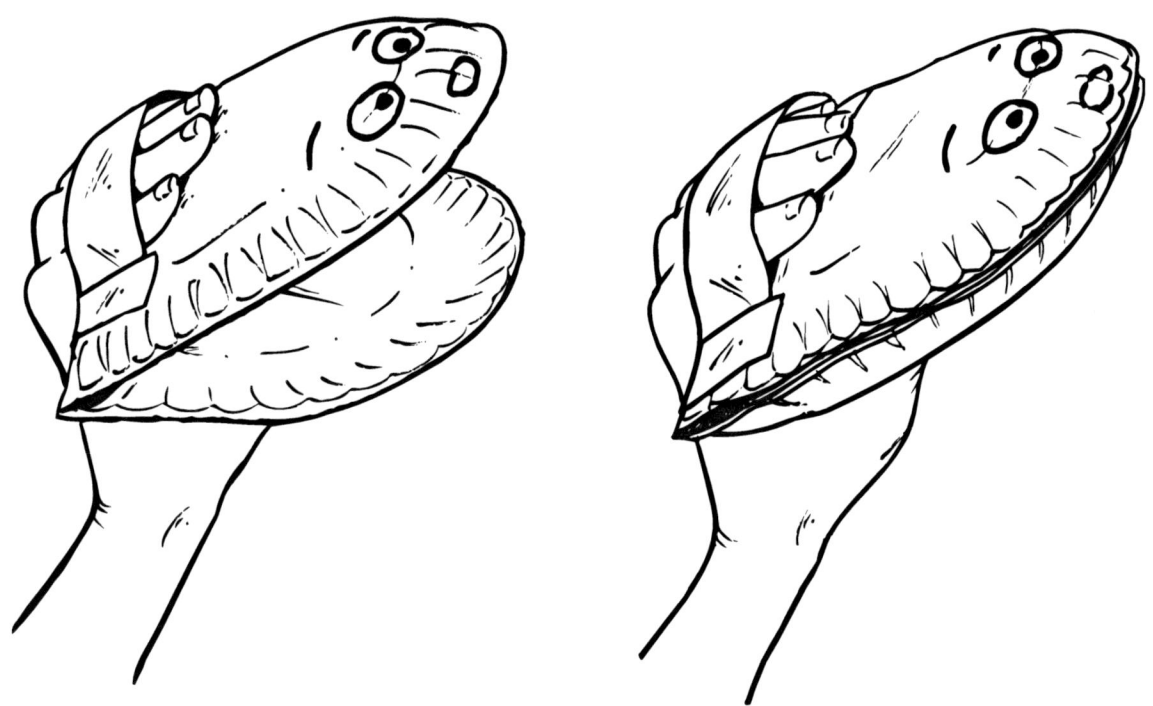

Some puppet mouths open and shut.

Children say words for puppets.

Children sing songs for puppets.

Concept: Puppet

Yes-No Questions

1. Are puppets toys?
2. Do children put puppets on their feet?
3. Do children put puppets on their hands?
4. Are some puppets little cars?
5. Are some puppets little animals?
6. Are some puppets little people?
7. Do some puppet mouths open and shut?
8. Can children say words for puppets?
9. Can children sing songs for puppets?
10. Do you have a puppet?

Wh- and How Questions

1. Who plays with puppets?
2. What are some puppets?
3. Where do children put puppets?
4. How do children make puppets talk?
5. How do puppets say words?
6. How do puppets sing songs?
7. What is a puppet?
8. What do puppet mouths do?
9. Who makes puppets say words?
10. What do children do with puppets?

Puppet Generalization Page

Circle the puppets. Put an X on each picture that is not a puppet.

Puppet Mini-Book

Copy this page. Cut apart the boxes on the dotted lines. Put the story in order to make a little book and staple.

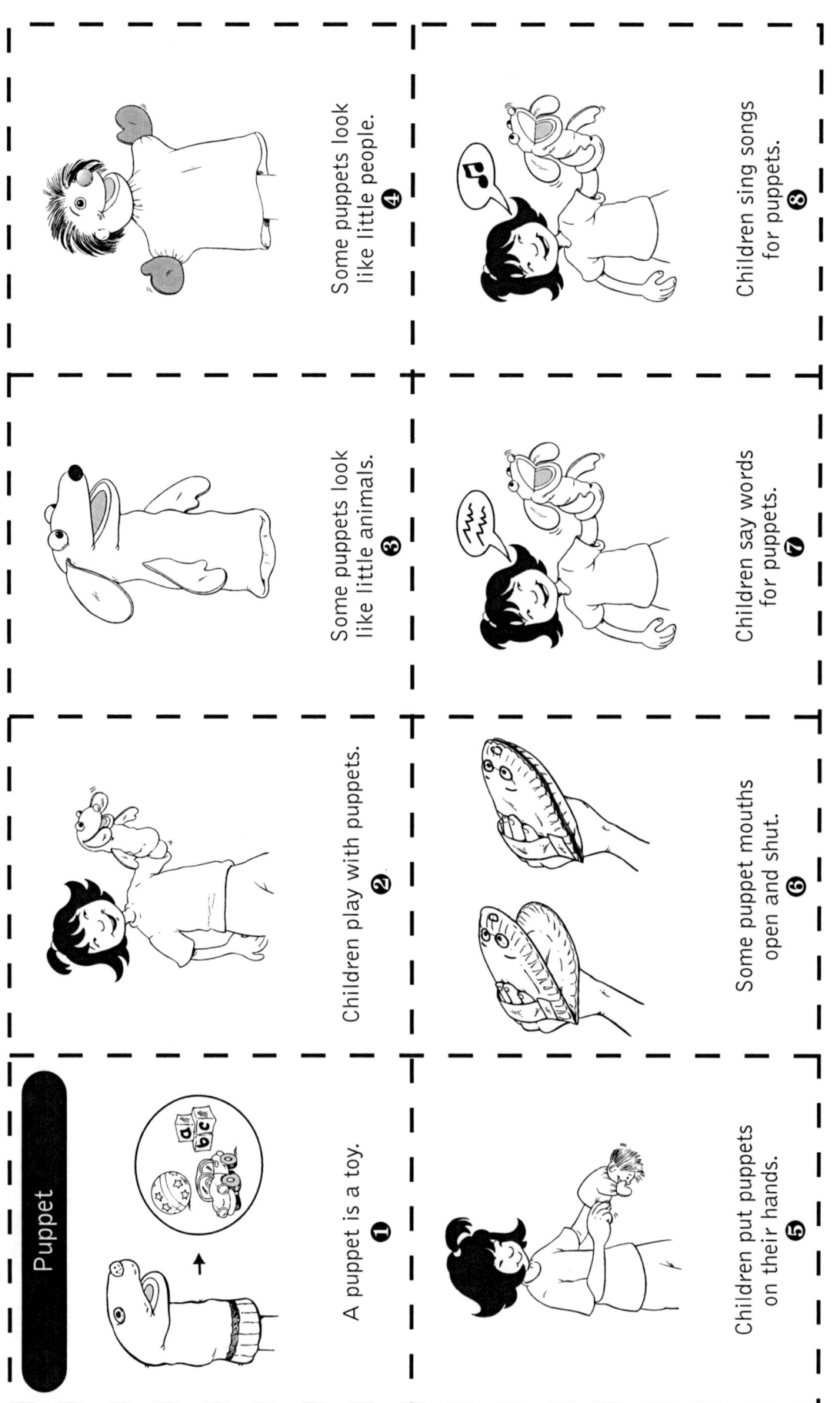

Puppet
Concept Development: Toys & Entertainment

Balloon

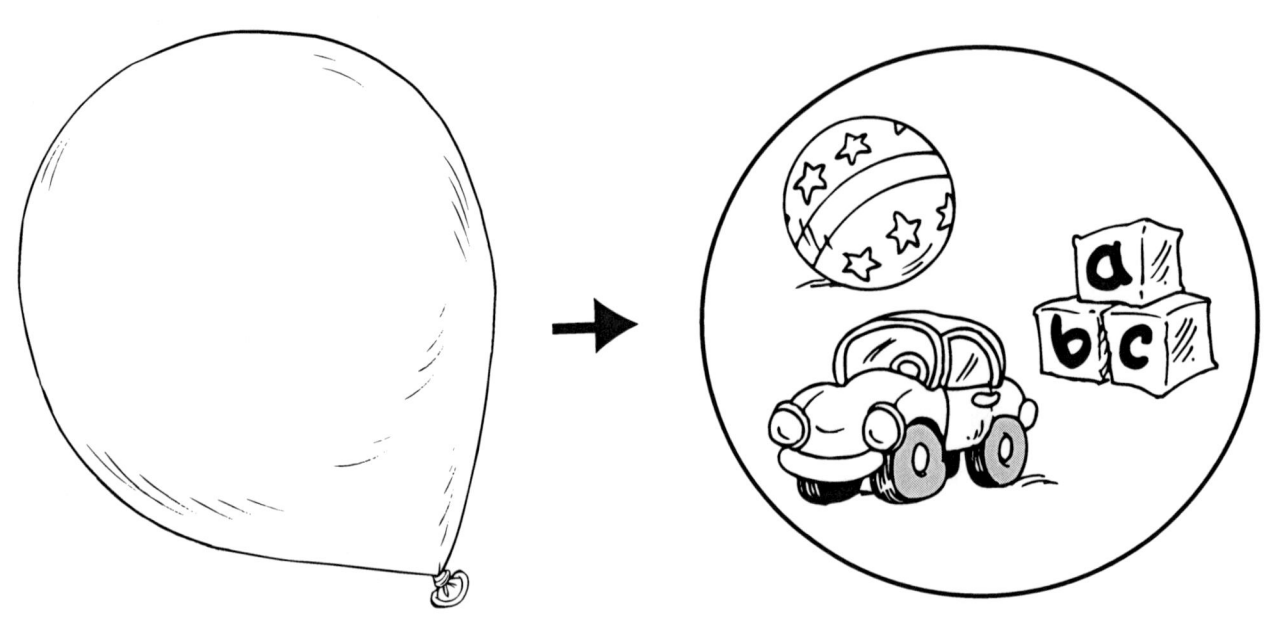

A balloon is a toy.

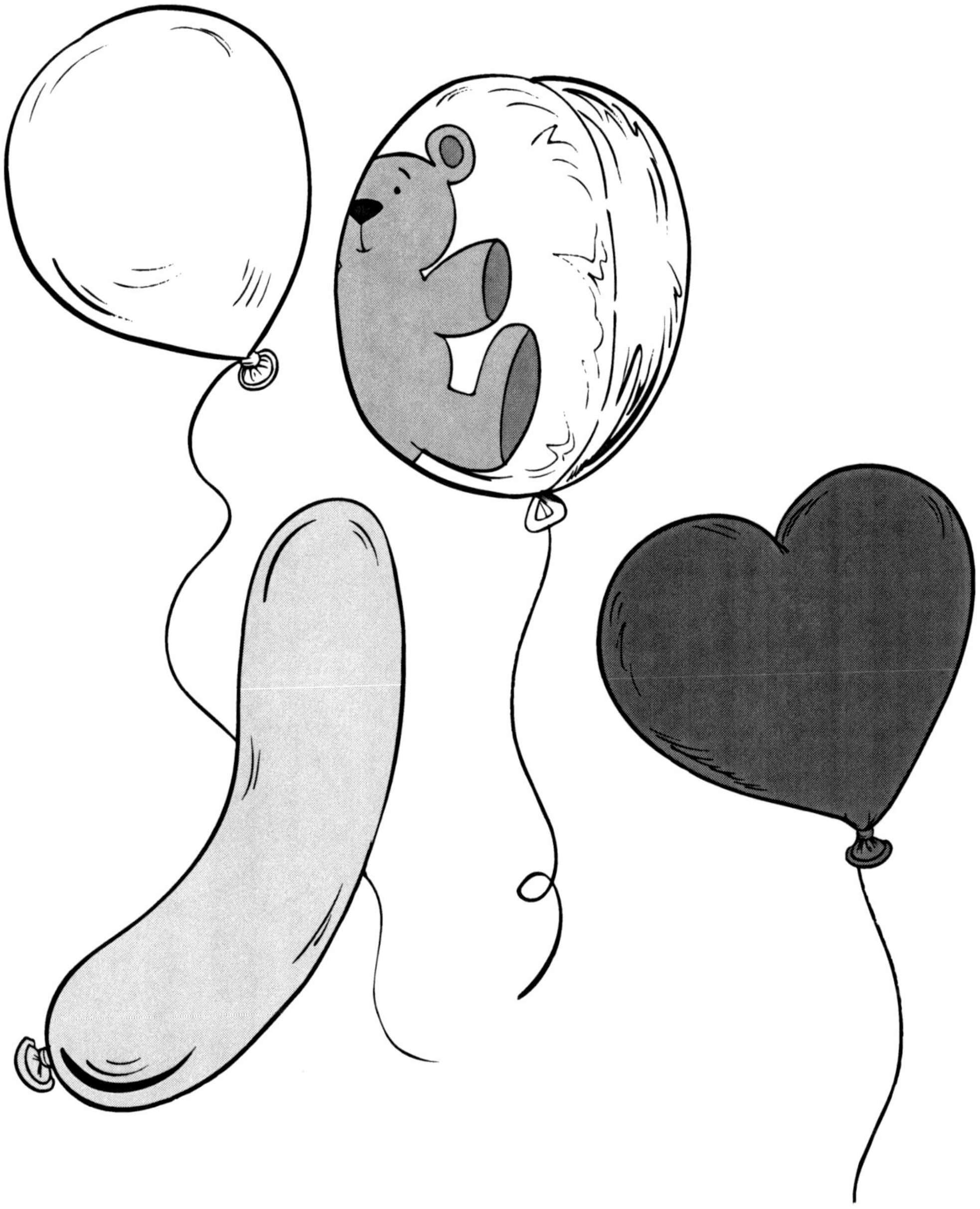

All of these are balloons.

  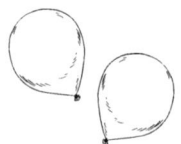

Children play with balloons.

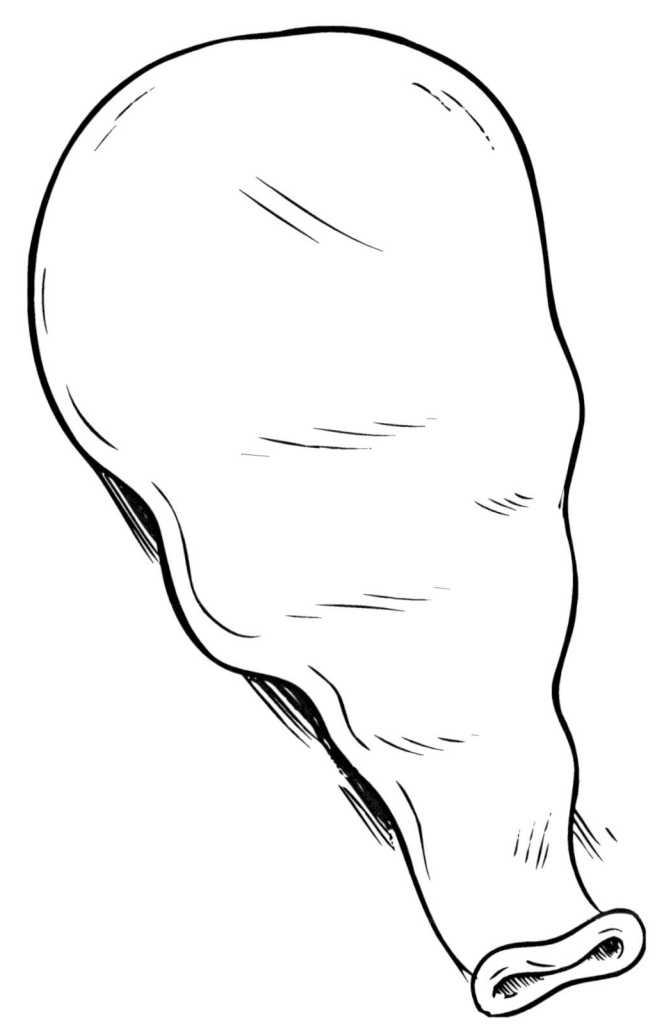

 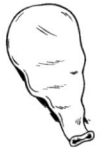

Sometimes balloons look flat.

  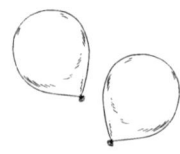

Children blow air into balloons.

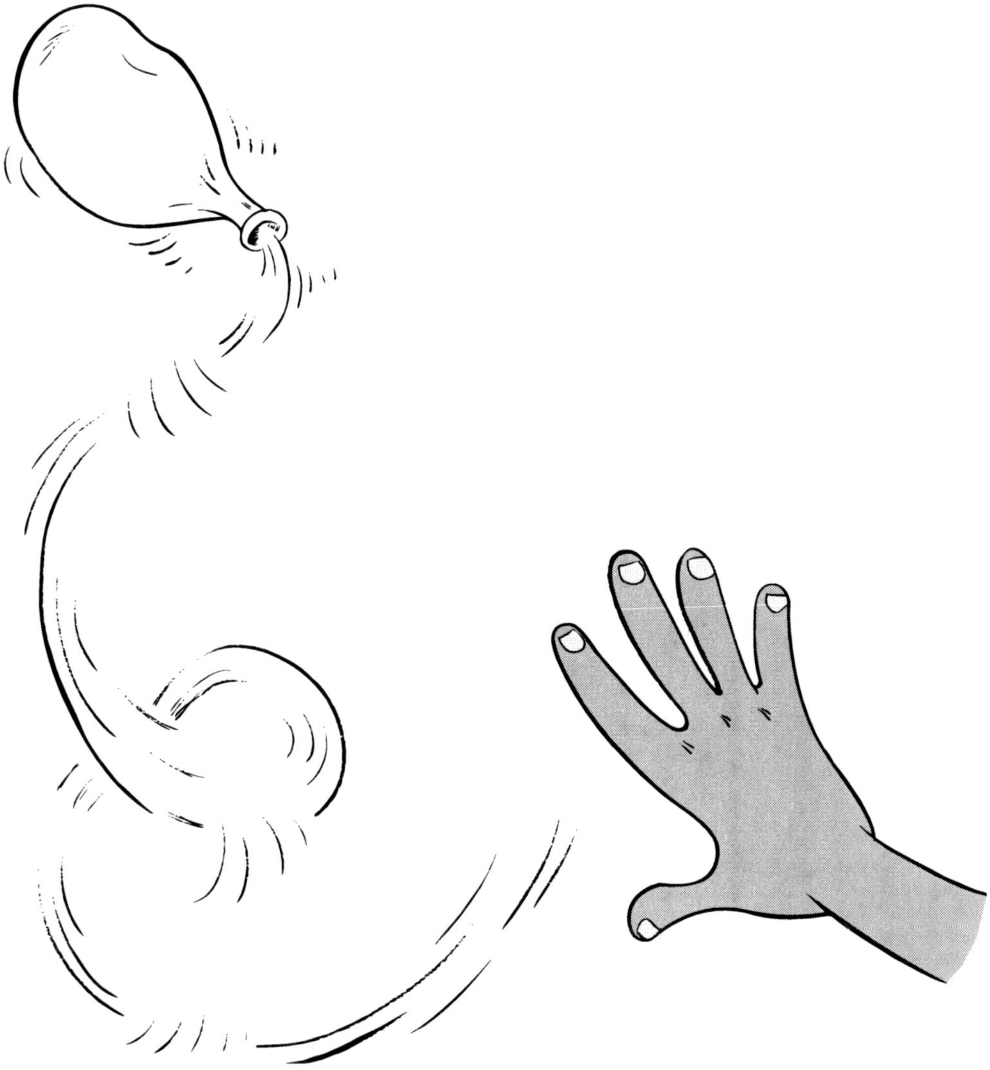

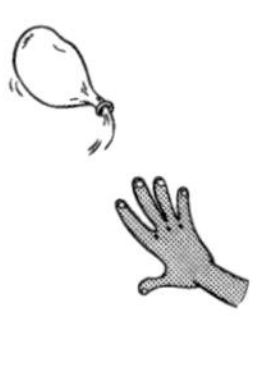

Let it go! The balloon will fly!

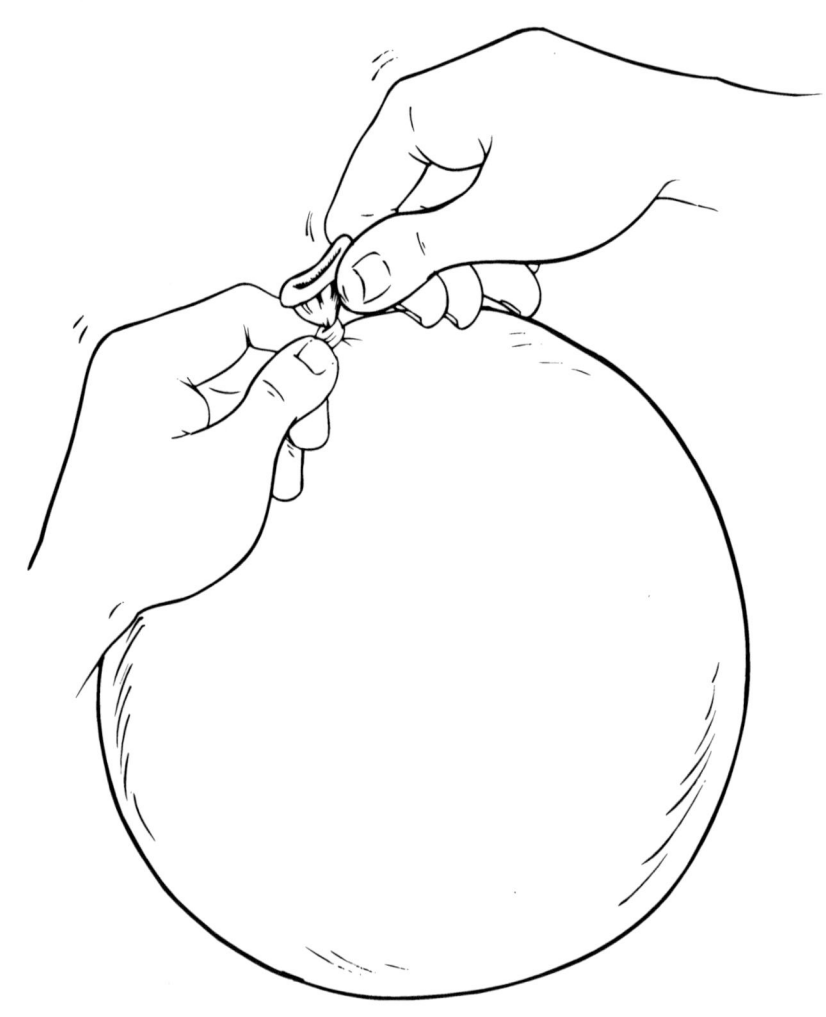

Tie a knot on the end to keep in the air.

Sometimes balloons pop.

Concept: Balloon

Yes-No Questions

1. Is a balloon a toy?
2. Is a balloon hot?
3. Do children play with balloons?
4. Can a balloon talk?
5. Can a balloon be round?
6. Can a balloon be flat?
7. Do you put dirt in balloons?
8. Do people drive balloons?
9. Do balloons pop?
10. Is a balloon something to eat?

Wh- and How Questions

1. What is a balloon?
2. Who plays with balloons?
3. How do you put air into a balloon?
4. What shape are balloons?
5. What do people put in balloons?
6. When is a balloon flat?
7. When is a balloon round?
8. What do children do with balloons?
9. How do you keep air in a balloon?
10. What happens when you let a balloon go?

Balloon Generalization Page

Circle the balloons. Put an X on each picture that is not a balloon.

Balloon Mini-Book

Copy this page. Cut apart the boxes on the dotted lines. Put the story in order to make a little book and staple.

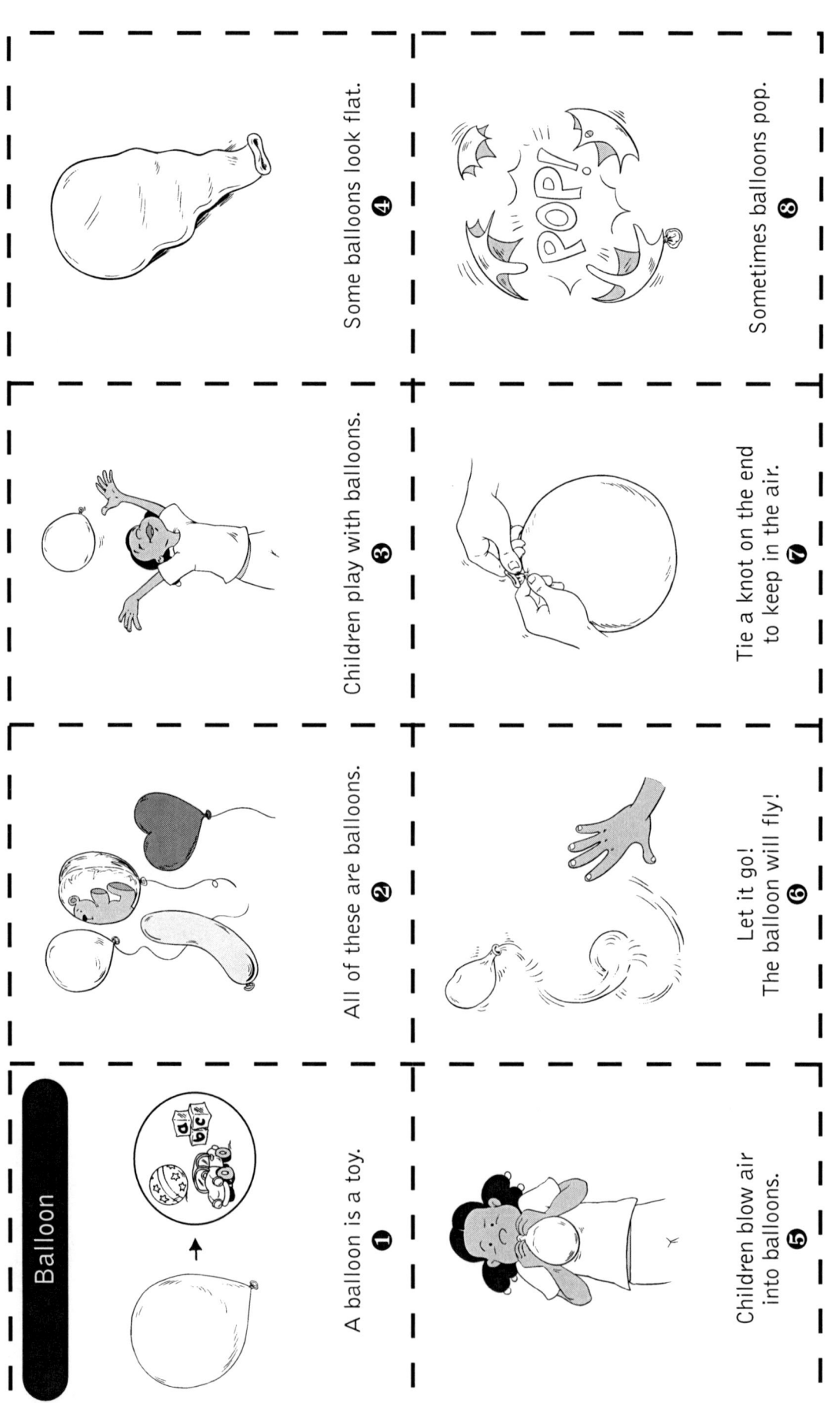

Sandbox

Children play in a sandbox.

A sandbox is outside.

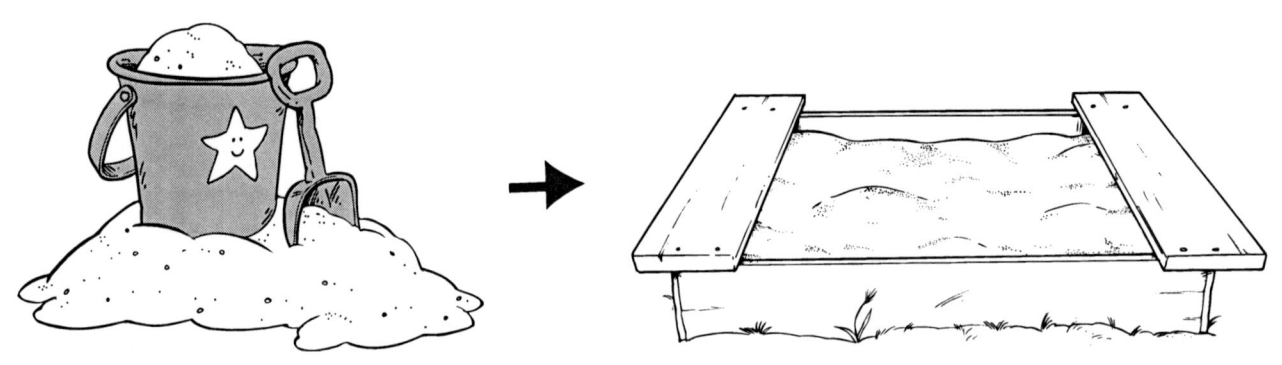

Sand is in a sandbox.

Children sit in a sandbox.

Children dig sand with shovels.

Children pour sand.

Children put sand in buckets.

Children dump out sand.

Concept: Sandbox

Yes-No Questions

1. Are rocks in a sandbox?
2. Is sand in a sandbox?
3. Is a sandbox in the bedroom?
4. Is a sandbox outside?
5. Do you dig sand with a shovel?
6. Do children put sand in food?
7. Do children put sand in buckets?
8. Do children pour sand?
9. Do children color with sand?
10. Can you dump out sand?

Wh- and How Questions

1. Where is a sandbox?
2. Where do children sit?
3. Who plays in a sandbox?
4. What is in a sandbox?
5. What do you do with a shovel?
6. Where can you put sand?
7. What can children pour?
8. What can children dump out?
9. Where do children dump sand?
10. How do you put sand in a bucket?

Sandbox Generalization Page

Circle the sand. Put an X on each picture that does not show sand.

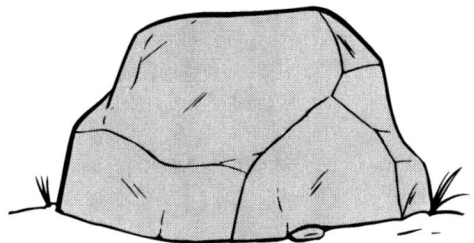
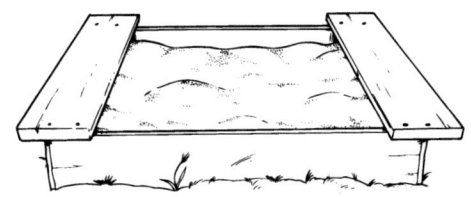

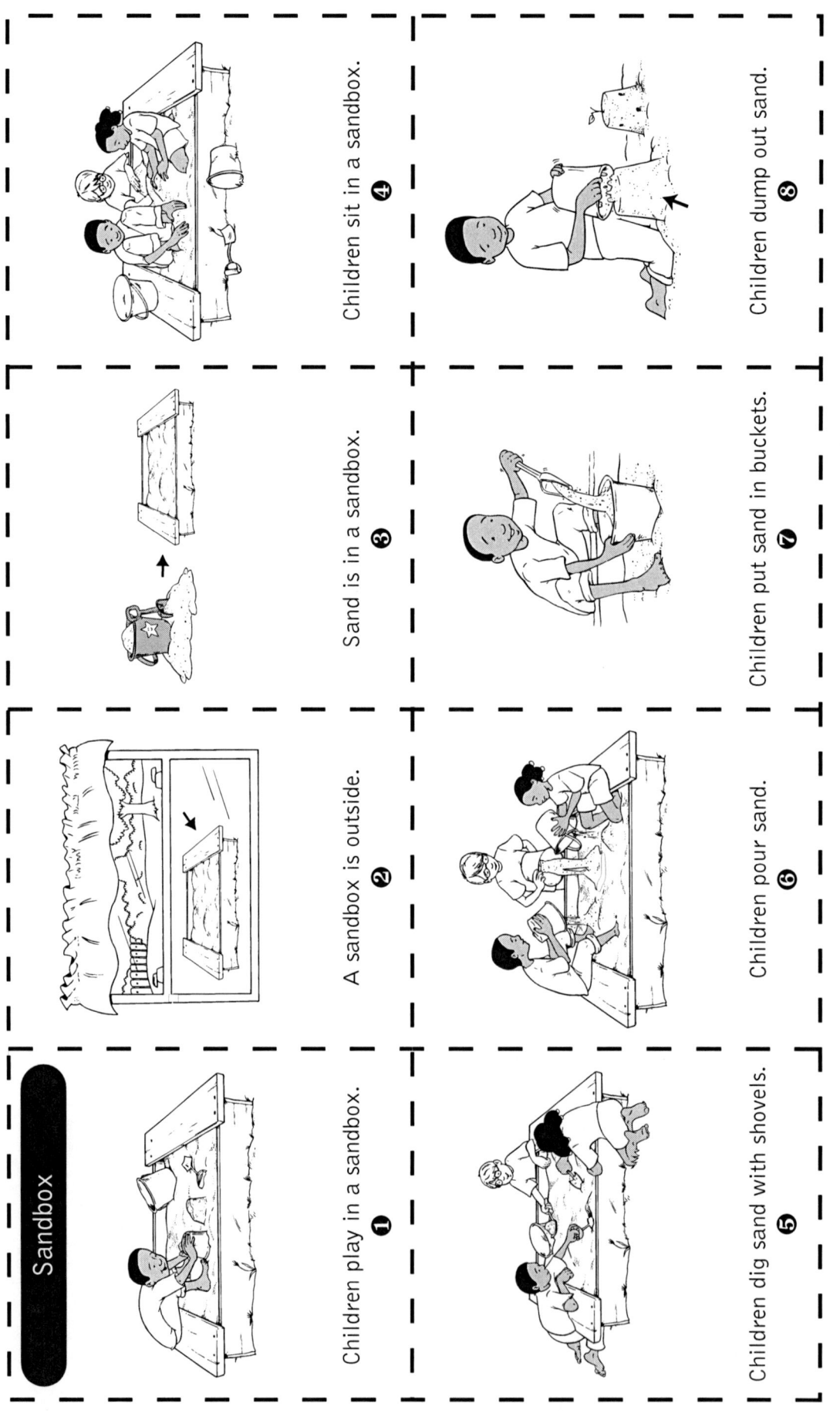

Swing

Children play on swings.

Swings are fun.

Swings are outside.

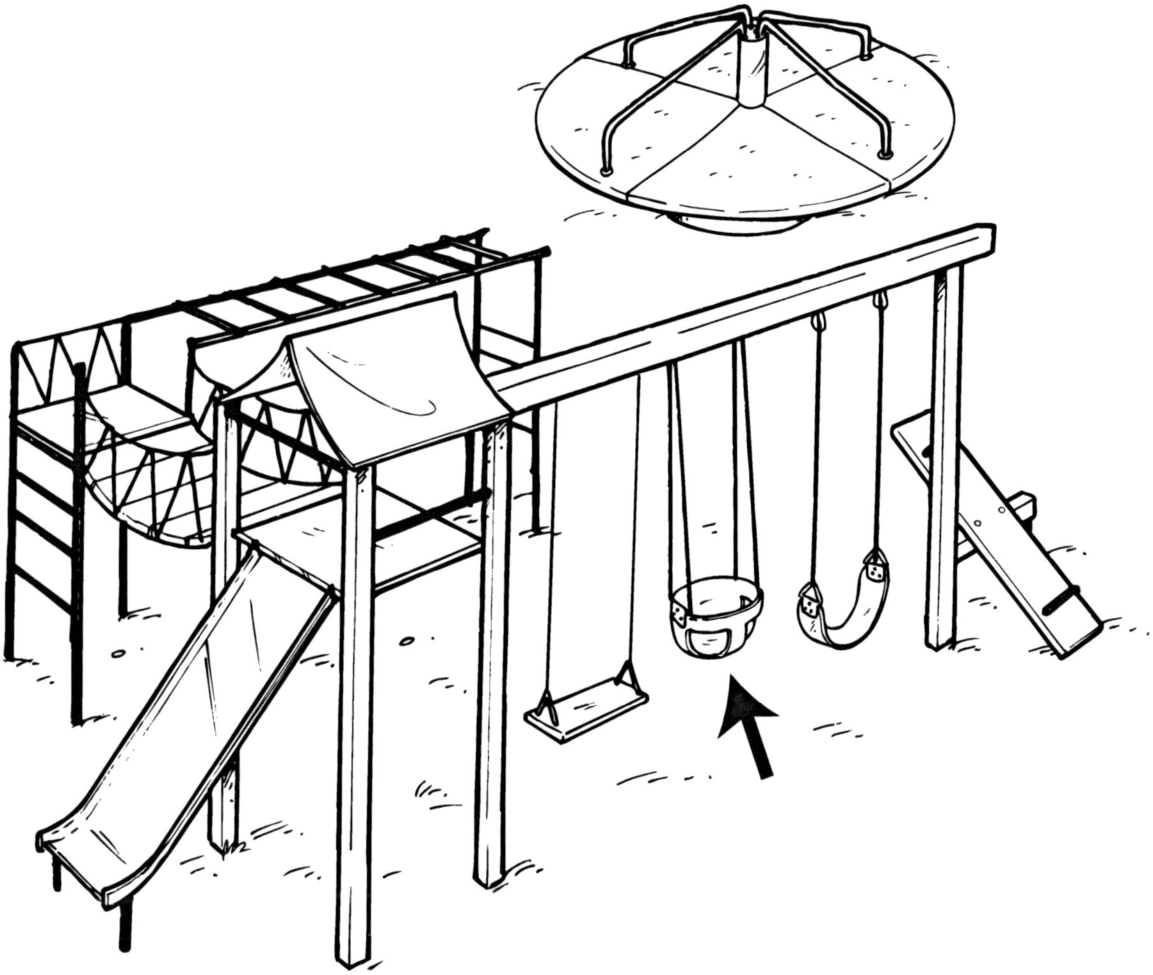

Swings are at playgrounds.

Sometimes swings are in backyards.

Children sit on swings.

Someone pushes the swing.

I can go up high in the air!

Concept: Swing

Yes-No Questions

1. Do children slide on swings?
2. Do children swing on swings?
3. Do children sit on swings?
4. Are swings inside?
5. Are swings at playgrounds?
6. Do swings stay up in the air?
7. Do swings go high?
8. Do people push swings?
9. Are some swings in backyards?
10. Do you like to swing?

Wh- and How Questions

1. Who plays on swings?
2. Where are swings?
3. Why do you push swings?
4. Where do children sit?
5. What goes high in the air?
6. When do swings go high in the air?
7. Who pushes swings?
8. Where are swings at school?
9. Where are swings at home?
10. What makes a swing go high in the air?

Swing Generalization Page

Circle the swings. Put an X on each picture that is not a swing.

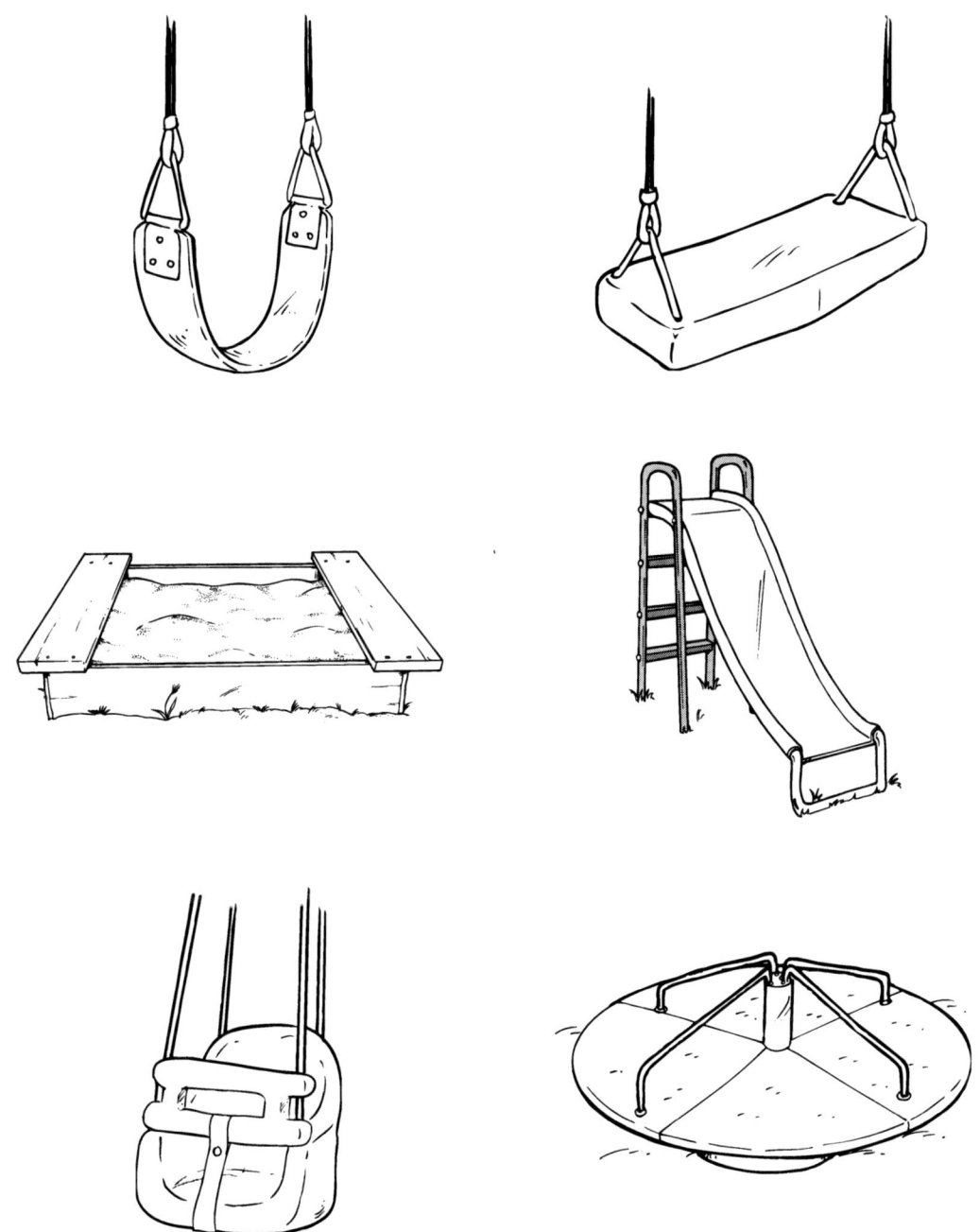

Swing
Concept Development: Toys & Entertainment

Swing Mini-Book

Copy this page. Cut apart the boxes on the dotted lines. Put the story in order to make a little book and staple.

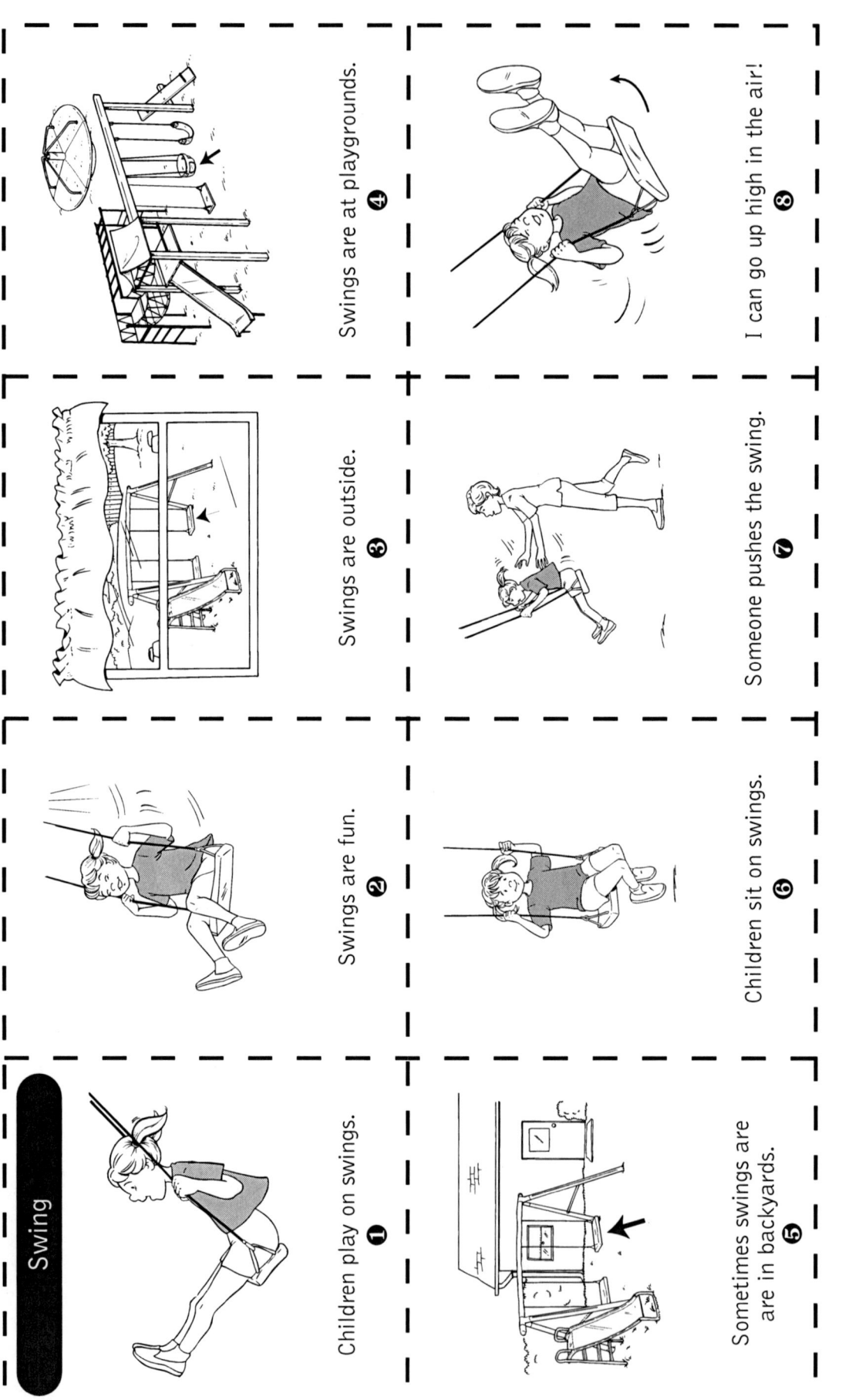

1. Children play on swings.
2. Swings are fun.
3. Swings are outside.
4. Swings are at playgrounds.
5. Sometimes swings are in backyards.
6. Children sit on swings.
7. Someone pushes the swing.
8. I can go up high in the air!

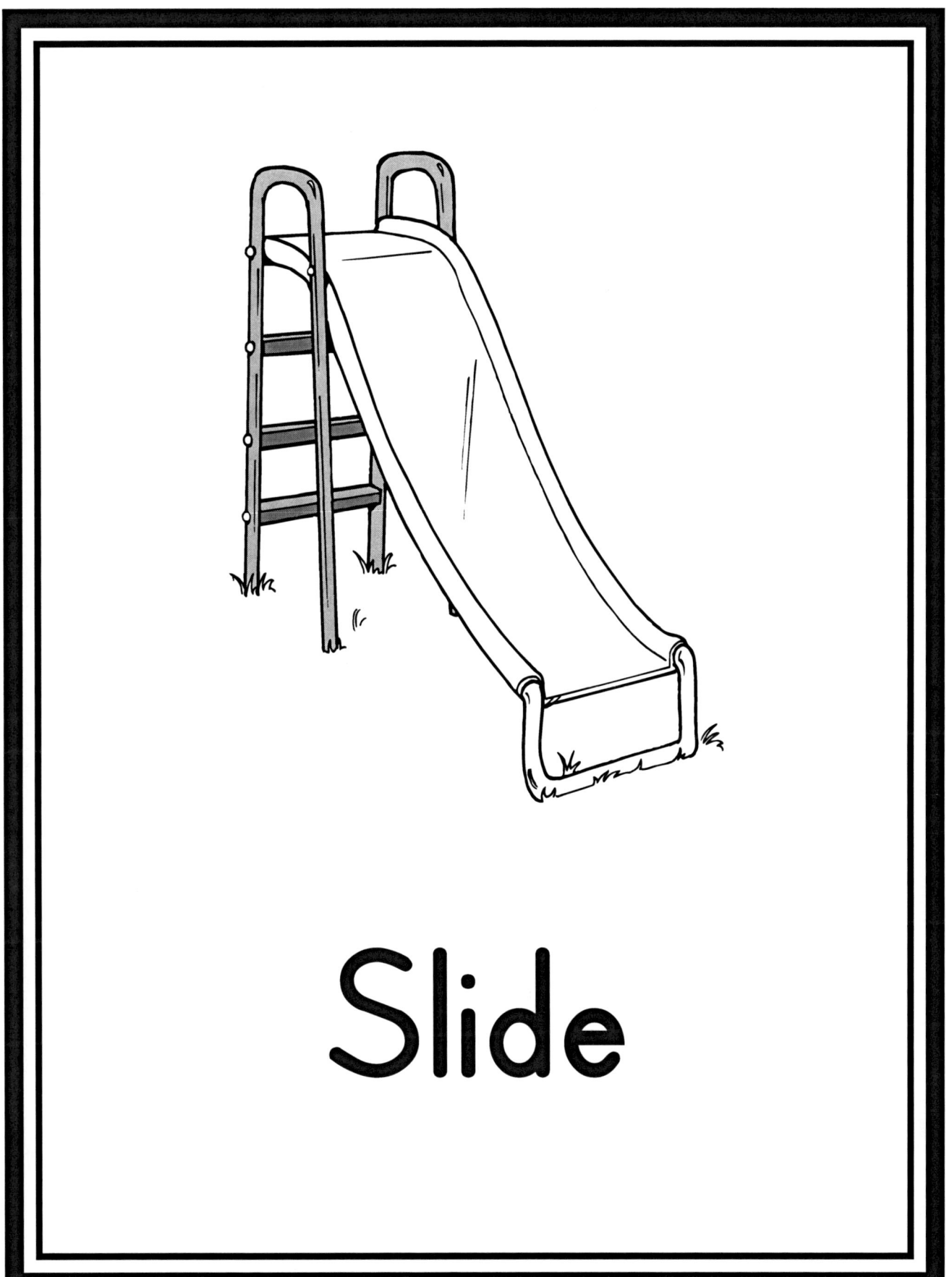

Slide

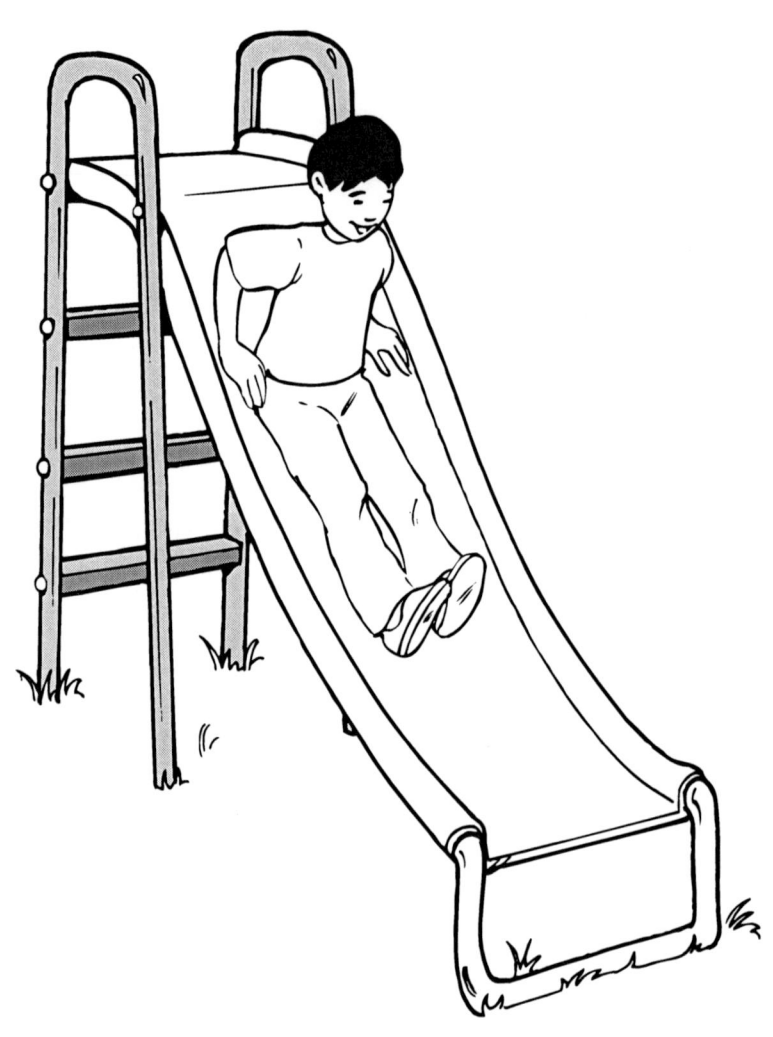

Children slide down slides.

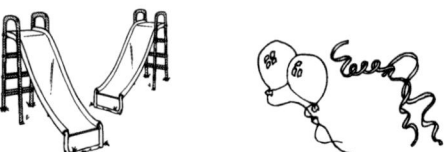

Slides are fun.

Slides are outside.

Slides are at playgrounds.

Sometimes slides are in backyards.

Children climb the ladder.

Children sit on the top.

Children can slide down fast to the bottom!

Slide

Concept: Slide

Yes-No Questions

1. Are slides furniture?
2. Do children play on slides?
3. Are slides in the kitchen?
4. Are slides at playgrounds?
5. Do children swing on a slide?
6. Are there ladders on slides?
7. Can you climb on a slide?
8. Do you slide slowly on a slide?
9. Do you slide fast on a slide?
10. Do you like to slide?

Wh- and How Questions

1. Who plays on slides?
2. Where are slides?
3. Who climbs on slides?
4. Why do children play on a slide?
5. How do you get to the top of a slide?
6. What do you do when you get to the top of a slide?
7. Where do children sit on a slide?
8. How do children slide down?
9. What do children climb?
10. Why do children climb the ladder?

Slide Generalization Page

Circle the slides. Put an X on each picture that does not show a slide.

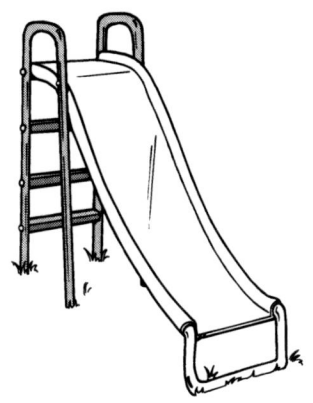
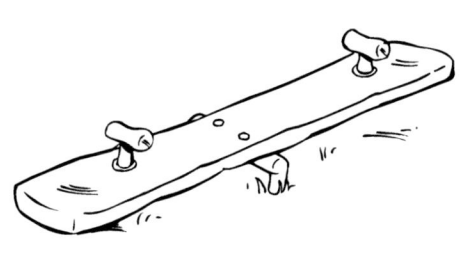
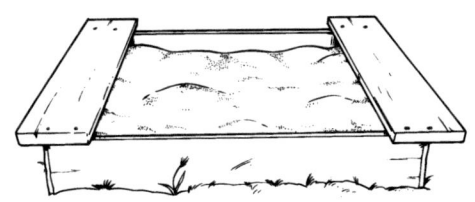

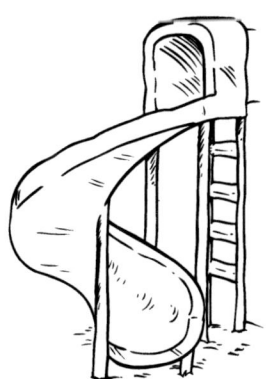

Slide Mini-Book

Copy this page. Cut apart the boxes on the dotted lines. Put the story in order to make a little book and staple.

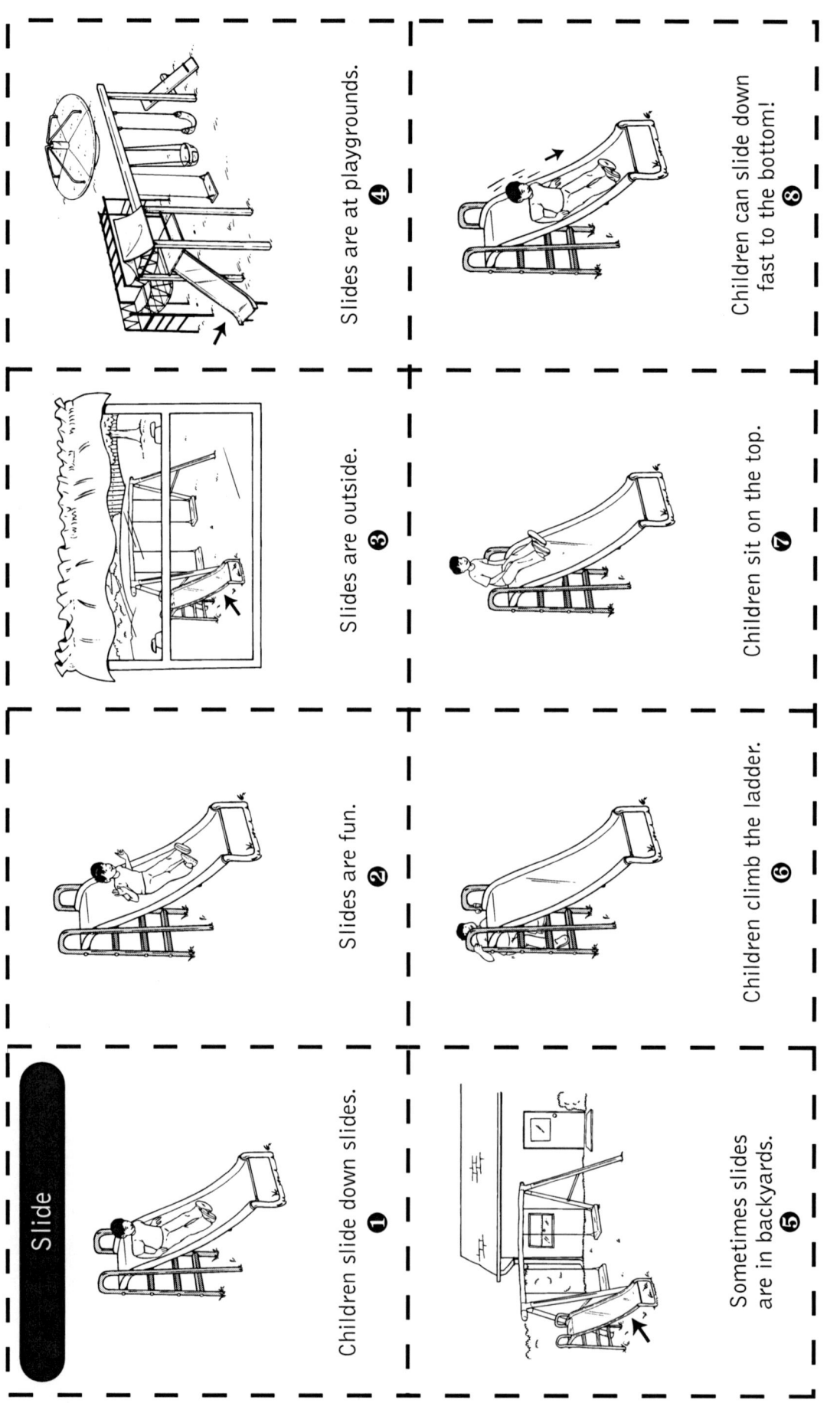

Slide

① Children slide down slides.

② Slides are fun.

③ Slides are outside.

④ Slides are at playgrounds.

⑤ Sometimes slides are in backyards.

⑥ Children climb the ladder.

⑦ Children sit on the top.

⑧ Children can slide down fast to the bottom!

Ball Activity: Ball Play

Materials: small, soft ball (or a favorite ball)

Begin rolling the ball back and forth. Once rolling is established, teach other ball actions like catching, kicking, and throwing, one at a time. Be careful not to rush through this part. For generalization, use different sizes and types of balls once the actions have been established.

Concept Development: Toys & Entertainment — Copyright © 2001 LinguiSystems, Inc.

Doll Activity: Wash and Feed the Doll

Materials: small tub, water, washcloth, soap, baby doll, bottle, baby bib

Fill the tub with water. Have the child wash the baby doll. Label the body parts as the child washes them. (You may need to start this activity hand-over-hand.) Then model feeding the baby doll the bottle. Prompt with "Feed the baby," "The baby is drinking," and "The baby likes milk."

Bubble Activity: Bubble Fun

Materials: jar of bubbles, soap, bubble gum, water, dishwashing soap, shallow aluminum tray, straws

Show the child bubbles from the jar, bubbles made with a bar of soap, bubbles in water, and bubbles blown with bubble gum. Encourage the child to pop and catch the bubbles. Then mix a small amount of the dishwashing soap in water (eight tablespoons of soap to a quart of water works well). Pour some of the soapy water into the shallow tray. Help the child put the end of a straw into the water and blow.* This will make lots of different sizes of bubbles.

* Only use this part of the activity with children who understand "to blow through the straw" instead of the usual "drink through the straw."

pop

catch

blow

blow

Block Activity: Build with Blocks

Materials: set of blocks (wooden or plastic), small toy cars

Help the child stack the blocks. Encourage her to stack the blocks as high as she can so the blocks will naturally fall. Take turns stacking the blocks. Then line up the blocks to make a road. Roll the cars along the road.

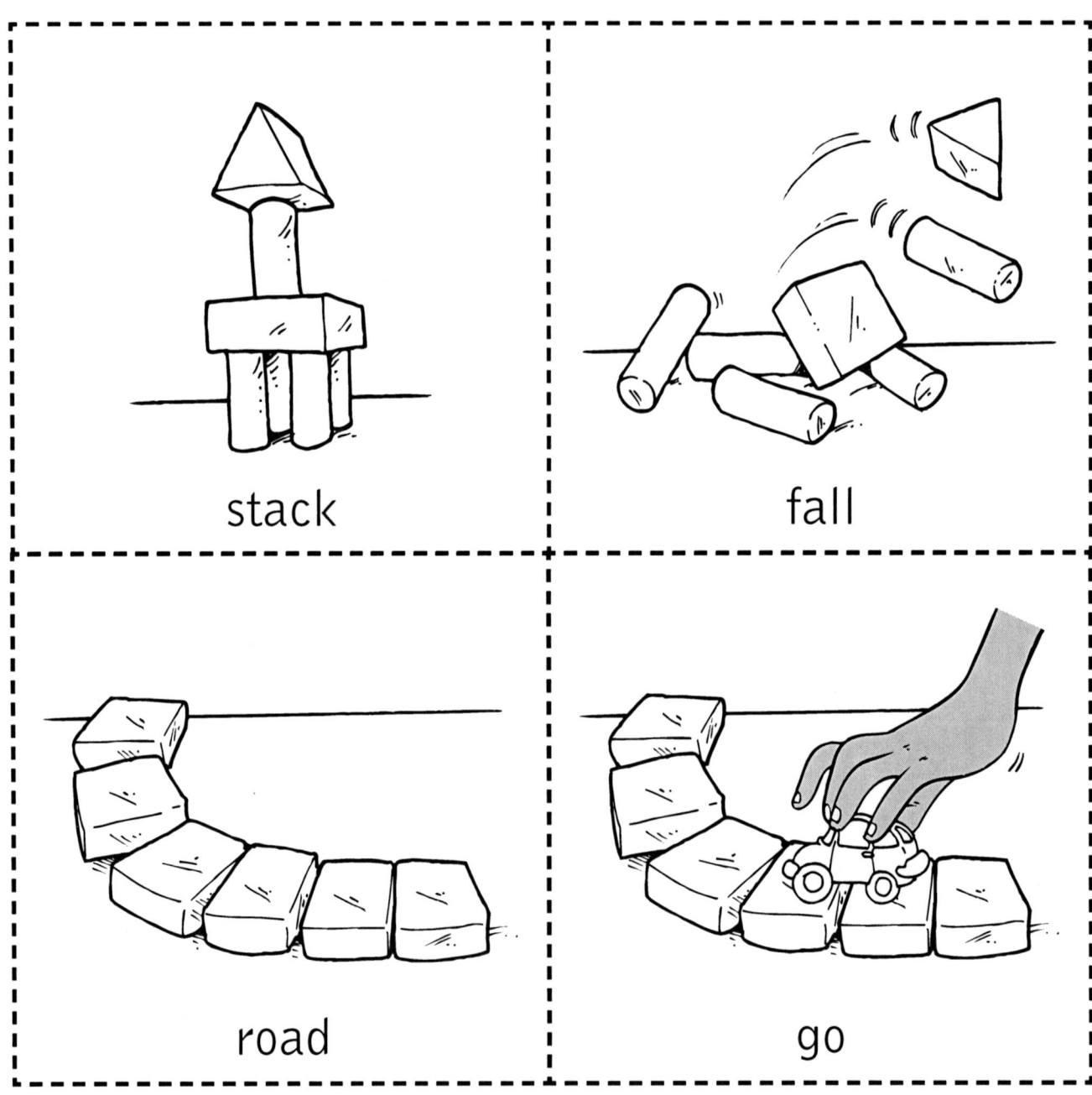

stack

fall

road

go

Concept Development: Toys & Entertainment

Play Dough Activity: Make Play Dough

Materials: 3 cups flour, 1½ cups salt, 6 tsp. cream of tartar, 3 T. vegetable oil, 3 cups water, food coloring, saucepan, measuring cups and measuring spoons, mixing spoon, stove

Mix ingredients and heat over medium heat. Keep stirring as materials form a ball. Remove from heat and let cool. Knead the dough as it is cooling. Store in an airtight container.

Play Dough Activity: Squish and Roll

Materials: play dough, rolling pins

Help the child gather up the play dough to form a ball. Then encourage the child to squish the ball of dough. Help the child use his hands to roll the play dough into a "snake." Then show the child how to use the rolling pin to make the play dough flat.

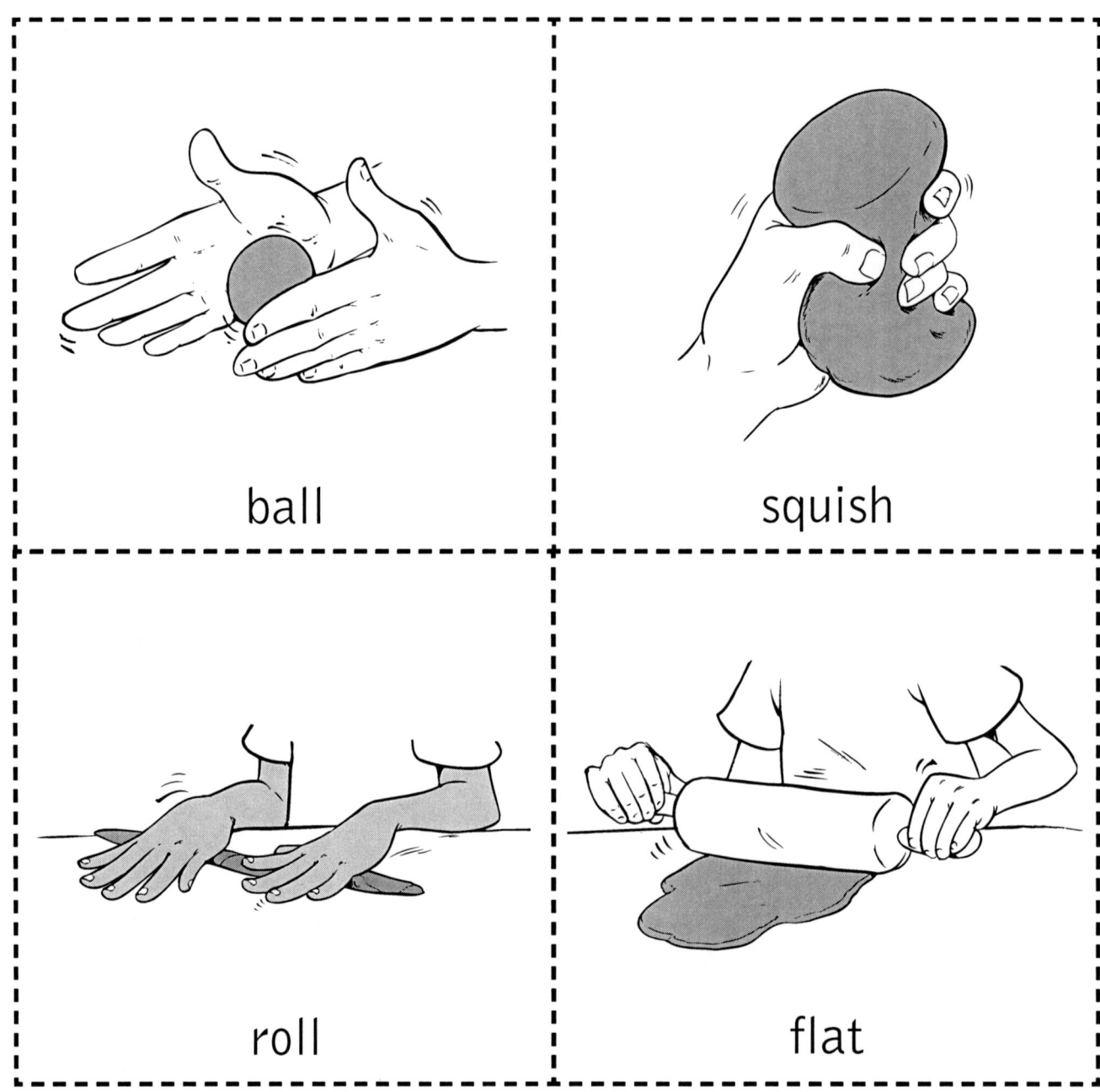

Puppet Activity: Talking Puppets

Materials: small paper plates, wiggle eyes, pom-poms, construction paper scraps, crayons or markers

Fold a paper plate in half (eating side of plate should now be in the middle). Decorate the top of the folded plate to make a face. Add a strip of paper to the top as illustrated to help child hold and move the puppet. By placing a hand through the strap, the puppet can "talk" or "sing."

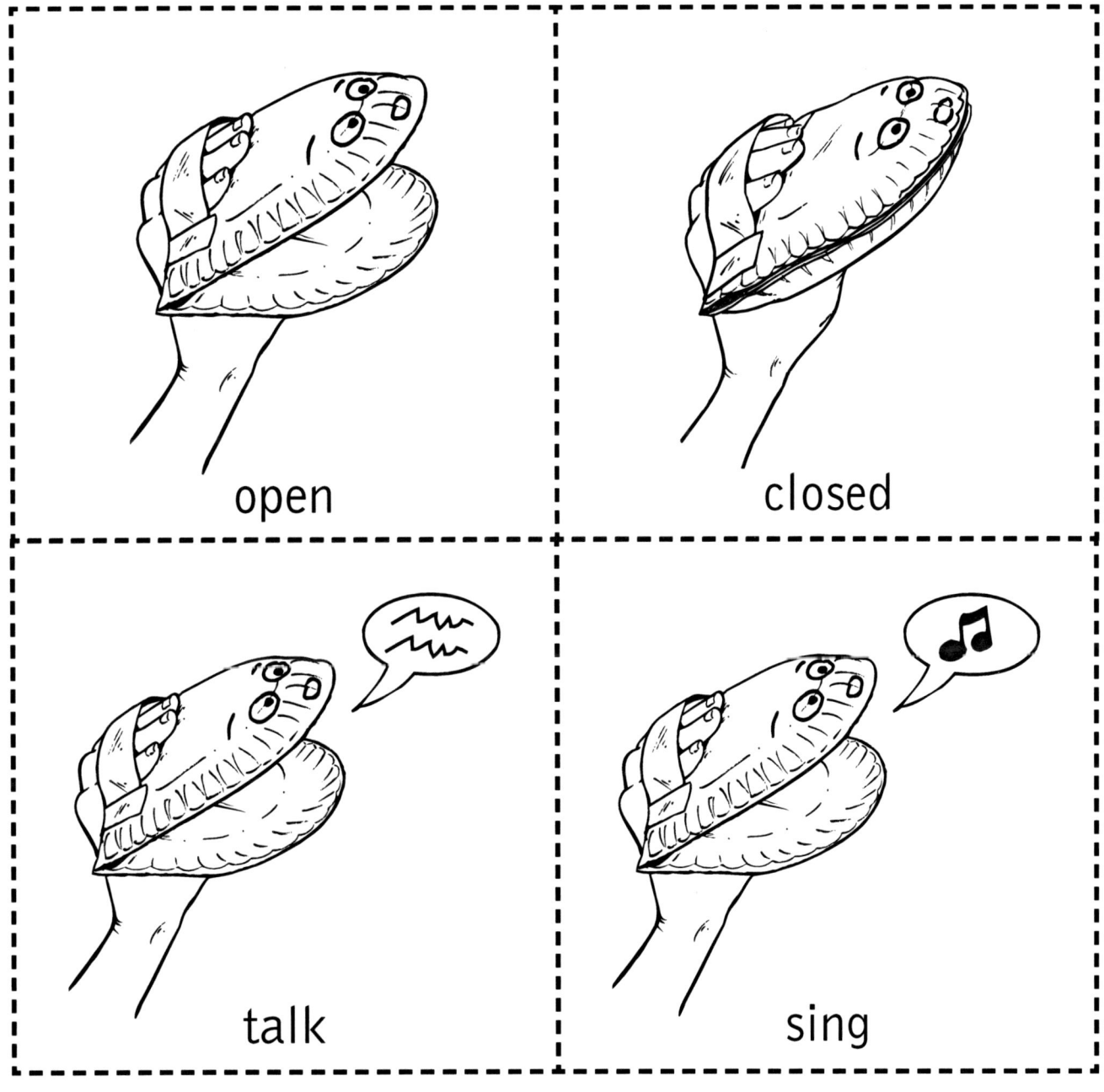

open

closed

talk

sing

Balloon Activity: Balloon Fun*

Materials: balloons of different shapes and colors

Blow up a balloon and let it go. Direct the child's attention to the balloon as it flies around the room. Blow up the balloon again and tie the end. Hit the balloon in the air. Encourage the child to take turns hitting the balloon with you.

*Caution: Be careful that the child does not put the balloon into her mouth. Also, some children may have latex allergies.

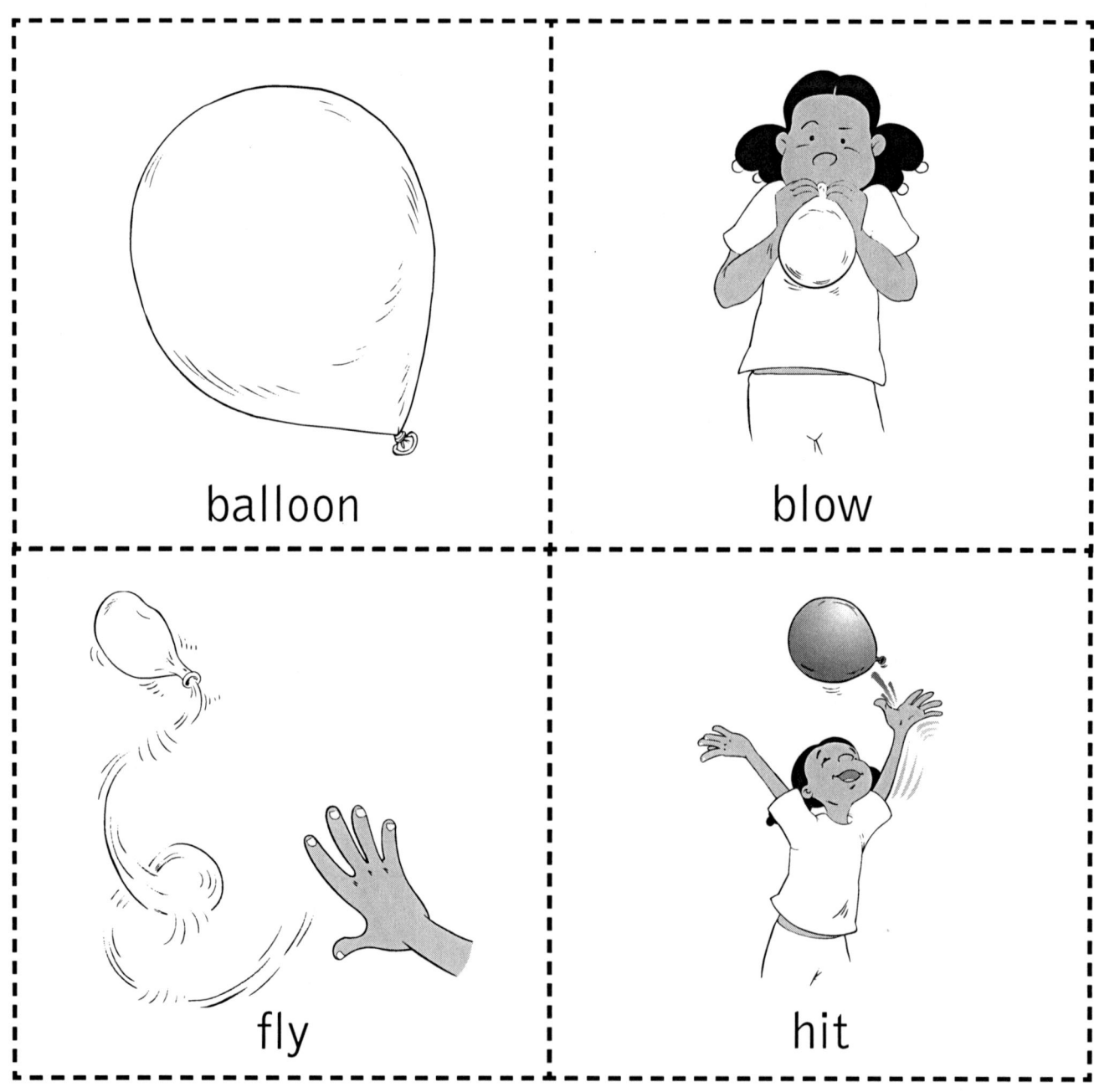

Sandbox Activity: Sandbox Play

Materials: sandbox, sand table or container of sand, plastic shovels and scoops, variety of cups or small containers, funnel

Help the child use the shovels and scoops to fill the small containers. Show the child how to dump the sand to make a mound. Use the funnel to fill other containers.

dig

scoop

dump

pour

Swing Activity: Learn to Swing

Materials: a swing set

Go outside to the swing set. If the child is fearful, have the child sit on your lap, facing forward while you swing. If the child is not afraid, have the child sit on the swing. Push gently from behind. Some children may need to be pushed on the swing several times before moving on. Others may be ready for prompts like: "Legs out!" and "Legs under!"

Suggested Literature

Toys and Entertainment
The Playground by Judy Thau
Baby's Toys by Neil Ricklen

Bubbles
Bubble Trouble by Mary Packard
The Baby Bubble Book by Rhoda Josephs
Bubbles Everywhere by Gloria Bancroft

Blocks
Building with Blocks by Jillian Cutting

Play Dough
Playing with Dough by Rigby Publishers

Puppets
Puppets for a Play by Rigby Publishers

Sandbox
In the Sand by Rigby Publishers